THRIVING
IN THE FIGHT

A SURVIVAL MANUAL
FOR LATINAS ON THE
FRONT LINES OF CHANGE

DENISE PADÍN COLLAZO

BK

Berrett–Koehler Publishers, Inc.

Berrett-Koehler Publishers, Inc.
1333 Broadway, Suite 1000
Oakland, CA 94612-1921
Tel: (510) 817-2277
Fax: (510) 817-2278
www.bkconnection.com

ORDERING INFORMATION

Quantity sales. Special discounts are available on quantity purchases by corporations, associations, and others. For details, contact the "Special Sales Department" at the Berrett-Koehler address above.

Individual sales. Berrett-Koehler publications are available through most bookstores. They can also be ordered directly from Berrett-Koehler: Tel: (800) 929-2929; Fax: (802) 864-7626; www.bkconnection.com.

Orders for college textbook / course adoption use. Please contact Berrett-Koehler: Tel: (800) 929-2929; Fax: (802) 864-7626.

Distributed to the U.S. trade and internationally by Penguin Random House Publisher Services.

Berrett-Koehler and the BK logo are registered trademarks of Berrett-Koehler Publishers, Inc.

Printed in the United States of America

Berrett-Koehler books are printed on long-lasting acid-free paper. When it is available, we choose paper that has been manufactured by environmentally responsible processes. These may include using trees grown in sustainable forests, incorporating recycled paper, minimizing chlorine in bleaching, or recycling the energy produced at the paper mill.

Cataloging-in-Publication Data is available at the Library of Congress.
ISBN: 978-1-5230-9250-5

33614082224717

First Edition
27 26 25 24 23 22 21   10 9 8 7 6 5 4 3 2 1

Book producer and text designer: Happenstance Type-O-Rama
Cover illustration: Ana Teresa Rodriguez
Cover design: Alvaro Villanueva

To my bizabuelita
Gregoria "Goyita" Miranda

Full Circle

During the war,
Uprooted from your land,
You found a way,
To raise your girls.

In the fourth generation,
One returned,
To reclaim what was taken.

Your fire and love live on in me.
Because of you, I can thrive.

CONTENTS

FOREWORD

I love the words and they loved me back.

SONIA SANCHEZ

T o watch Denise create this book was like living in this quote from Sonia Sanchez. There are so many powerful messages that Denise "loved" and shared in her homage to Latinas, and to all those who are "Thriving in the Fight."

Denise is the perfect narrator to illuminate the fight for equity and justice. She has been in this fight—and knows about "Thriving in the Fight" because she has been there. Denise is an activist, a strategist, a campeona. She is a woman of firsts—integrating family and work as a pioneer leader in a national faith-based organization. We know that the "first" is the one who pushes the boundary, who blazes a path for her sisters on the road behind her. As Denise is in the fight, we see so many of her strengths—her resilience, foresight, and bravery. These strengths are all aspects of Denise that are drawn on as she creates this powerful homage to brave Latinas.

Thriving in the Fight speaks directly to and about the experiences and lives of Latinas. Our sisters have been ignored; more than that, they have been made invisible in the larger discourse. This book fills an important gap, shines a light on a space that many didn't know existed. As I read the book, I was drawn in by three messages that I continuously encountered. There were themes that spoke to me: using voice, acting authentically, and being strategic. Denise speaks of the necessity for Latina women to raise their voices, to make sure that they are visible, to move to the center from the corners to which they have sometimes been relegated. Denise also shares the importance of authenticity, of not letting your true self be smothered, covered over. I was blown away by Denise's integrity in her acknowledgment of the racism against Blacks that is present in the Hispanic community. This kind of authenticity, this willingness to tell the truth even when it is difficult, is one of the distinctions that characterizes *Thriving in the Fight*. Denise is incredibly ardent in her resolution that those who are successfully progressing are strategic in acting as champions against battles and conflicts that adversely affect their communities. In each chapter, Denise talks about the importance of not surrendering, of not giving up—pushing through when the road seems incredibly treacherous.

Another amazing mujer sabia, Elizabeth Acevedo, offers the following words:

> **Write the stories you've always wanted to read. Allow yourself to become the main character of your narrative. Become both the window and the mirror for those who read your book.**[1]

With her literary contribution, Denise provides both a window for and a mirror to the many Latinas who are drawing from *Thriving in the Fight* to strengthen their armor and prepare to win well in the battle for justice, equity, and freedom.

DR. STACY BLAKE-BEARD,
Visiting Professor,
Tuck School of Business
Dartmouth College

INTRODUCTION

HOW CAN YOU THRIVE AND
FIGHT AT THE SAME TIME?

My first fight lesson happened when I was in elementary school. Daddy gave me an important piece of advice. He said, "If a girl ever calls you out to fight after school, just punch her in the nose right then and there. Don't wait until after school where she will have all her friends and family to make the fight unfair." This might seem to you like strange advice to give a little girl. He was passing along hard-earned intel he'd gathered from his childhood growing up as one of the first Spics to move to the South Bronx, New York, in the 1940s. He ran fast from the neighbors' hate for the new, big, loud Puerto Rican family on the block.

Hermana, I'm telling you this story because while, thankfully, I've never had to act on Daddy's schoolyard advice, I have spent most of my adult life fighting on the front lines of change to make our communities places where Black, Latino, and all children of color and their families can thrive. This work of activism and organizing communities is critically important for the success and survival of our children and families. Because of how important this work is, we need you to be part of the fight for social, racial, economic, and political change.

Throughout the book, I will mostly use the word Latina to mean people who identify as women and are of Hispanic or Latino descent. Most people of Hispanic/Latino descent first identify by their country of origin. I will mostly default to Latina, but will occasionally use the terms Hispanic, Latino, and Latinx. Latinx is a gender-neutral term designed to acknowledge and honor the intersectionality of our people and our culture.

Women of Color's Bodies Are the Front Lines of Change

A great many of the people doing the work in the fight for social, economic, political, and racial change are women of color.

Black women, Latinas, Asian sisters, Pacific Islanders, First Nations women, Southeast Asians, and many others serve as the bones that hold the flesh of our families, communities, and institutions together. You serve as room moms, school board members, clergy members, elected officials, spiritual guides, community organizers, activists, and healers who serve daily in countless unnamed and often unpaid positions of leadership.

I'm writing to tell you that I see you.

The work you do is very important. You're not alone, and what you're experiencing is not only happening to you.

Finally, I want you to know that those of us who are fighting on the front lines of change need you in the fight.

> **Women of color's bodies are the front lines of change.**

You, my sister, are not just fighting with children and families who are being most harshly impacted by our nation's greed, neglect, and disregard for young lives. You are not just fighting on the front lines with families facing our nation's blatant disregard for Black lives. Your bodies are the front lines of change. Women of color's bodies *are* the front lines of change.

Our Country Is Leaving Our Children Behind

It is only when our Black children are free, that I am free. When our Black children are made whole, I am made whole. Until America acknowledges its racist roots and digs out all its vestiges, this country will not be whole. Until Latino children are no longer targeted by the police or separated from their families by harsh immigration enforcement, none of us are whole. Until I acknowledge the ways I participate in and help uphold systemic racism, I will not be whole.

You don't need to look very far to see examples of how we are leaving our country's most vulnerable children, elders, and families behind. Children and families who have the darkest skin are being told to fend for themselves while white billionaires and major corporations gorge themselves on tax breaks and giveaways amounting to trillions of dollars.

In Flint, Michigan, a generation of Black children have been poisoned and will experience lifelong health problems because their well-being was not a priority to public decision-makers. During the COVID-19 global pandemic, Latino families experienced disproportionate unemployment. The country as a whole had more unemployed people than during the Great Depression of the early 1900s. In the US the epidemic disproportionately infected and killed Native Americans, Black people, Latinos, and darker skinned members of the Asian community. At the same time, Black men and women were being hunted down and killed in broad daylight by white vigilantes and police officers who served as prosecutor, judge, and jury—resulting in a pattern of modern day lynchings.

Yet You Have Audacious Faith

Despite the fact that your opponents are brutish and well financed, you, my sister, face these challenges with courage, righteous anger, and creativity. You endure the pain of grief and loss that pushes you beyond your limits. Yet you have audacious faith in yourself and in your community's capacity to make a difference. You keep pushing and you keep fighting. And each time you win, you uncover a thousand more battles to fight.

The work of making social change is hard. Waking up every day to take on the most pressing issues of our time is both exhausting and exhilarating. The work of building power in communities through activism, community organizing, and protest can be exhausting because it often demands long hours and includes crises that erupt on weekends, during vacation, and on every news cycle. Because you're a leader, when people aren't sure what to do, they call you. The work of catalyzing change is also exhilarating because when you think you can't have another conversation or write another word or have another protest, something starts to move and you can feel it. Suddenly all the groundwork you and your community have laid starts to shift the narrative, change the policy, and move the will of powerful people. You feel the joy and beauty of our full humanity when you shout together with the rest of the world: "No Justice, No Peace," and "Somos más, y no tenemos miedo."

Perhaps you have been a leader in your community for many years. Maybe you've joined the fight for change recently. Or, you may be trying to figure out how to plug in. Wherever you find yourself on the path toward justice, we need you in the fight through thick and thin.

What Does Thriving in the Fight Mean?

Thriving in the fight means being active, being engaged, and passionately contributing 100 percent of your brilliance to bringing about social, economic, political, and racial equity in this country.

There are many ways to be part of the movement for change. Sometimes you find yourself working from a place of joy and flow.

That's thriving. Other times, you wonder if you'll make it to the end of the day. That's probably more like surviving. See figure 1.

For example, if you've been in the work for a while, you may find yourself *staying* in the fight yet not getting the results for which you'd hoped. Other times you feel that you are barely *surviving* in the fight. At times you may be *winning* important victories with and for your people. Yet you are doing so at a tremendous cost to your body, psyche, personal relationships, and maybe even your career.

© Denise Padín Collazo

FIGURE 1. Moving from surrendering to thriving

On any given day you might find yourself moving along many parts of this spectrum, and that's real. In this book, I'm inviting you to go beyond *staying* in the fight, *surviving* in the fight, or just *winning* in the fight. In it, I invite you to explore what changes you need to make so that you can spend as much of your energy as possible *thriving* in the fight for social, racial, economic, and political justice. Think of it as a guidebook to taking your leadership and impact to the next level.

How Will This Book Help You?

I am writing this book from my perspective as a straight, light-skinned, US mainland–born Puerto Rican woman.

If you are a **Latina change agent**, I've literally been in your shoes. This book will provide you with relatable stories about the ups and downs of my journey. I hope they bring you not only encouragement but concrete tools for how to have greater impact.

If you identify as **Black or Afro-Latina**, this book can serve as a guidebook to better understand your light-skinned Latina sisters and some of the roots of their cultural limitations (not excuse, just understand). You may find the chapter on disrupting anti-Blackness within the Latinx community to be of particular interest.

If you are a **person in the work of trauma and healing**, this book will help you consider ways to care for yourself as you care for others.

If you identify **anywhere along the racial and gender spectrum and seek to support, develop, and systematically center the leadership of Latinas and women of color** more broadly, you will find the experiences and exercises in this book a helpful investment in your development. You can use the ideas within to change institutions in which you participate. Because in institutions where Black and Brown women thrive, everyone thrives.

Finally, if you consider yourself to be an **anti-racist ally** to Latinas and women of color more broadly and seek ways to encourage all women of color to succeed, this book will help you learn ways to clear a flight path for some of the most brilliant leaders of our time.

Women of Color Carry Outsized Responsibility

If there is one thing I know, it's that in the movement for social change, women of color produce. They deliver a top-notch product. They usually get the job done, no matter what.

That, my sister, is also part of the problem.

You see, as a Latina, it's likely that you carry outsized responsibility both at work and in your personal life. Yet, you rarely have the commensurate resources, recognition, or room for reflection to get the job done. You get the job done anyway—often at a tremendous cost to your family, personal relationships, career, or body. In order to set Latinas and all women of color up for suc-cess, they need equal doses of resources, responsibility, recog-nition, and room for reflection. The unsustainable load and the unsustainable pace of social change work leads too many Latinas to leave the fight.

If you are thinking about leaving, please don't.

We need you.

Today, there are not enough Latinas and other women of color in top positions in the fight for change. Too few Latinas and Black women lead labor unions, community organizations, community organizing networks, political campaigns, philanthropies, and nonprofits in general.

Yet Whites Have Outsized Authority

Despite recent advances, in the world of community, economic, and political change in the US, Latinos are woefully underrepre-sented in leadership. A recent survey conducted by the Center for Effective Philanthropy received responses from fifteen thousand executive directors.[1]

75% identify as White

9% identify as African-American or Black

6% identify as Hispanic or Latinx

4% identify as Asian

3% identify as multiracial

1% identify as American Indian or Alaskan Native

4% identify as Pacific Islander or Native Hawaiian

1% identify as a race/ethnicity not listed above

Latinos make up 18.3 percent of the United States population, totaling 59.9 million people.[2] If Latino nonprofit executive leader-ship were commensurate with their representation in the popula-tion, they would hold 18.3 percent of the top leadership positions in the nonprofits surveyed. Instead, they hold 6 percent. Based on the Center for Effective Philanthropy survey, 60 percent of respondents were women. It seems reasonable to estimate that about 3.6 percent of nonprofit executive directors are women of Hispanic descent.

Our Institutions Were Birthed in White Supremacy

Most change organizations and political campaigns have built-in structures that reinforce white supremacy. For example, in *Dismantling Racism*, Tema Okun defines some of the characteristics of white supremacy in organizations.[3] Later, we will list all the symptoms, but below are five symptoms (see figure 2). If you would like to cut out your own version of the card to carry around with you, see the "Resources" section at the end of this book.

FIVE SYMPTOMS OF WHITE SUPREMACY IN INSTITUTIONS

➤ individualism

➤ fear of failure

➤ fear of open conflict

➤ binary thinking

➤ right to comfort (for some)

Credit: *Dismantling Racism*, Tema Okun

FIGURE 2. Five symptoms of white supremacy culture in institutions

These systems and structures make it virtually impossible for women of color, and people of color more broadly, to show up as their full, most creative selves.

In contrast to these five symptoms of white supremacy (individualism, fear of failure, fear of open conflict, binary thinking, and the right to comfort for some), many of our strongest leaders of color have a collective vision, not just one based on individual achievement. Latinas can see many ways to make change, not just one way. Many are bold enough to risk failure for the chance to win. They value truth-telling, not secrets. They share leadership and lift up others, and by doing this, they create a whole that is even more brilliant and mesmerizing.

> **Yet, when you walk into spaces that weren't built for you, you show up as a smaller version of yourself.**

Mujer, I've seen how you show up to family gatherings—all flashy, gorgeous, and clear about your role. Yet, when you walk into spaces that weren't built for you, you show up as a smaller version of yourself. Unless you're careful, you find yourself melting deeper into your chair when you're in a corporate boardroom or a donor's grandiose living space. When you show up in multiracial spaces, you're usually relegated to the back of the room, or you put yourself there on purpose. In moments when you do try to make your point, you may find yourself having to assert your leadership over and over to be heard. Rev. Traci Blackmon is one of the most prophetic religious leaders of our generation. She serves as associate general minister of Justice and Local Church Ministries for the United Church of Christ and senior pastor of Christ the King Church in Florissant, Missouri. She once said to me,

> People used to say I found my voice when Ferguson happened. I tell them that's not when I found my voice, that's when people started listening.

Like Rev. Blackmon, you have something to say. Your voice must also be heard if we are to have a chance at freedom. You know your community like no one else, yet your leadership is not centered in the movement for change. You are often sent to meetings to be the brown face to represent your organization. There are times when you propose bold new strategies and receive little more than a polite nod from others—then crickets. Sometimes you let this slide. Other times, you take great risks to be taken seriously. At times your voice is not heard no matter how loudly you shout.

I know some of you can relate to being given a big title but little real decision-making power. I call that fake power. Sometimes you wonder if you have been hired to be your company's hood ornament. Smile, look pretty, show up out front, then put your head down and do the work. This is not the path to liberation.

You are asked to bring your community and people into strategies that don't make sense to you. Those strategies were often developed by people that Steve Phillips describes in his book *Brown Is the New White* as "smart-ass-white-guys" thousands of miles away from your community.[4] You've been hired to work in the "field" (how ironic) to implement strategies you had no say in creating. These outsourced strategies are irrelevant, and you know they won't work. Yet, you mute your voice or it gets muted for you. Phillips blasts the Democratic Party for spending less than 2 percent of its 2010 and 2012 dollars on people-of-color-owned consulting firms. For example, when a new political candidate of color decides to run for office, they are often encouraged to hire or take direction from white consultants who design detailed campaign plans telling the candidate how to reach their own people. Even worse, some consultants advise the candidate to ignore their own natural constituents and focus on the ever-elusive white persuadable voters in their district.

Latinas Are Taught to Serve without Expecting Anything in Return

If you wonder why you defer to others, even though your gut is telling you something different, here may be a clue. Latinas and many other women of color have been taught by faith, family, culture, and tradition to be humble and serve without expecting anything in return. Women from many cultures are taught this subservience. Many times, in public, Latinas are most comfortable setting others up to shine and prefer to stay out of the spotlight. Yet, in private, it's the opposite. In private, it's women who bind us all together. Women bind our congregations, communities, and organizations together.

> **Latinas and many other women of color have been taught by faith, family, culture, and tradition to be humble and serve without expecting anything in return.**

Because of the important role you play in your world, dear sister, you will probably never stop fighting with and for your people. If you leave your current role, you'll find one that suits you better. Because you are gritty, I am inviting you to have more impact tomorrow than you do today. I'm inviting you to embrace your Alpha Latina self. The phrase Alpha Latina was coined and embodied by an unapologetically powerful leader and former member of the Nevada State Assembly, Lucy Flores. It means be your full self. Don't turn the volume down on your power or strength to make other people feel comfortable. I invite you to ignite your Chingona or baddest Latina self (to learn more, check out the excerpt of the great poem called "Chingona Fire" by Angela

Aguirre in chapter 5). It was passed along to you by the women who came before you. When you accept the power of who you are and stop shying away from it, you'll start walking into your fullest *badassery*. Your community needs your voice to be the central, driving force in the fight for change.

Three Keys to Thriving in the Fight

> To thrive in the fight, I'm inviting you to *lead* into your vision, *live* into the fullest version of you, and *love* past the negatives that hold you back.

In this book, I'll encourage you to continue to apply the best of your leadership to changing lives for our people. I'll share three keys to thriving in the movement for social, economic, racial, and political change. To thrive in the fight, I'm inviting you to *lead* into your vision, *live* into the fullest version of you, and *love* past the negatives that hold you back.

- ➤ **I'll encourage you to *lead* into your vision for the future.** Trust your gut. Do the work the way you know it needs to be done. When you have a vision of something new, go build it. Don't just wish for a future version of reality; we need you to lead us all into it.

- ➤ **I'll encourage you to *live* into the fullest version of you.** My comadre once said to me when I was fussing about my clothing size, "Can you just love your body?" I'm going to ask you the same question. Can you just love yourself? Will you accept your sizzle? Can you own it? Instead of wondering where your limits are, will you push yourself into new territory? Are you willing to leave behind some deeply embedded mindsets that may not serve you anymore? If you are, you'll find yourself doing things you once thought unimaginable. Look at me, I never would have imagined that I'd be writing a book. I believed I wasn't a good writer. As you push yourself past old boundaries and false beliefs, your impact will grow and your people will benefit.

➤ **I'll encourage you to *love* past the negatives that hold you back.** You've been told many things about yourself, about your leadership and your vision. Some of it comes from others, and some of it is internal to you. There are negative messages, negative people, and negative circumstances that limit you. Don't let that happen. Love past them. Don't wait for answers and permission to come from others. Many people will tell you your ideas are impossible, improbable, or impractical. Love yourself enough to push past the no's, the not-now's, and the not-yet's.

Three Warning Signs of Surrendering in the Fight

On the other end of the spectrum from thriving in the fight is surrendering in the fight. Surrender means giving up, or passively standing by while problems get worse. Leaders who have surrendered in the fight are passive. They tread water, follow the rules, and stay busy.

There are three tell-tale signs that you are surrendering in the fight. When you surrender you find yourself

➤ *wishing* for a future reality to emerge,

➤ *wondering* where your limits are, and

➤ *waiting* for permission and answers to come from others.

If you see the warning signs of surrender, don't worry; it can happen to anyone. Take some space to reflect on what needs to change for you to move out of that place of surrender. Reach out to a trusted colleague for help. Phone a friend, or do whatever you need to do to move from surrendering toward thriving.

I'm glad you're taking some time to invest in you and breathe with me. Along the way, we'll apply the thriving (lead, live, love) and surrendering (wish, wonder, wait) spectrum to the following areas of your leadership:

- Together, we'll consider how to **integrate family and work**. When I refer to family, I'm assuming that we are talking about people connected by both choice and blood.
- We'll discuss how important it is for you to **lead from the front**.
- We'll strategize about ways you can **disrupt anti-Blackness** within and beyond your culture of origin.
- I'll invite you to consider what it means for you to **lead clear on purpose**.
- I'll share lessons and invite you to consider new ways to **thrive by raising the money** you need to sustain your change-making work.

I've Been There

I've spent my adult life working to make the world a better place because I come from a long line of women who stared down impossible odds and won.

My great-grandmother Gregoria "Goyita" Miranda was kicked off her land in Puerto Rico when the father of her children died. She was left homeless and raised six girls by herself in the early 1900s.

One of these girls was Elisa Morales, my grandmother "Abuela Lela." When Lela was thirty-seven, she decided to leave a domestic abuse situation. One day her husband threw a heavy object at her and instead it struck her only daughter in the head. That was it. Lela had been willing to tolerate the abuse herself, but she would have none of it for her kids. Shortly thereafter, she boarded a diesel boat and started the process of relocating herself and her six children to New York City. She raised them alone by working days in a garment factory and nights at Bellevue Hospital.

Years later, I grew up in the farm town of Castroville, California. After school, when I'd bust through the mobile home door, I could smell what Abuela Lela was doing before I could see her. She was chopping the ingredients for sofrito, which was the base of whatever wonderfulness that would be served up for dinner that night. Abuela didn't think much of herself, but she was a winner and a change agent. Her love changed my whole family history. Her love got me all the way to Harvard University. On graduation day, I imagined myself standing on her tiny shoulders.

> **Love yourself enough to push
> past the no's, the not-now's,
> and the not-yet's.**

My experience at Harvard exposed me to what real wealth looks like. My classmates would take skiing trips during holidays— to Switzerland! Once I graduated, I knew my work would be in the streets with people like Abuela, Daddy, and perhaps your people too. Together with others, I've helped build Faith in Action (formerly PICO National Network), the country's largest faith-based community organizing network, which consists of three thousand congregations and forty-five community organizations in twenty-five states, the District of Columbia, Puerto Rico, and countries across the globe, including Haiti, Rwanda, and El Salvador.

Community organizing is an approach to advocacy that results in material change in people's lives. Community organizing is people centered. Individuals, communities, and institutions come together, share their experiences, and conduct people-centered research and analysis. Then they focus their collective power and shared systemic analysis to force decision-makers to make changes that benefit the most vulnerable children and their families.

I was the first woman to give birth, raise a family, and stay on as a full-time professional organizer for my national organization. Before me, women would often enter the organization in their twenties and move on once they were ready to start a family. Juggling family and work has been my reality for my entire career. My daughter Elisa grew up attending community canvasses and actions. As I wrote this book, my grandbaby Leyla Rose was building underwater worlds with her colorful sea-life toys. As a result of my experience and the experience of many other women, I've spearheaded an innovative family-work integration policy at Faith in Action that centers on the needs of Black women who are often the most marginalized people in the workplace and often have the most caregiving responsibilities outside the workplace. The policy centers the needs of women of color, yet benefits all staff.

When I lived in San Francisco in the 1990s and early 2000s, as director of the organization now called Faith in Action Bay Area, I led a citywide coalition that won more affordable housing units for the city's most vulnerable residents. We were the first organization to model for the Faith in Action network how to use voting and ballot initiatives as a tool for winning change. Yet, at first, whether it was because of my youth or my gender, or because I had a toddler at home, I was overlooked by the organization and network leaders as a candidate to serve as director of the organization. Despite the fact that I had become a very successful community organizer, I had to push my way forward to even be considered for the role.

In 2009, I helped Faith in Florida (formerly PICO United Florida) lead a statewide ballot campaign with groups such as the Florida Education Association, New Florida Majority, AARP, and faith leaders from across the ideological spectrum. Together, we defeated Florida's Amendment 3 in November 2012, which would have decimated funding to schools and basic services. Yet a year later, I realized that the executive director of PICO United Florida had been taking credit for my work with his board of directors. Despite the fact that I had led the ballot measure to victory and helped raise millions of dollars for the measure and the organization, many of his board members didn't even know my name—let alone what I had done.

By the time I was promoted to chief of staff of the national network, I had raised $50 million for the work of organizing. In 2016, I led our national voting program, which held over eight hundred thousand face-to-face or on-the-phone conversations with voters, 80 percent of whom were regularly ignored Black, Latinx, and Asian/Pacific Islander voters. Our contact with voters in states around the country fueled changes like paid sick leave and state minimum wage increases for workers, millions of dollars for transit improvements, funding for pre-K education, and other changes that benefit millions of the most vulnerable kids and families every day.

Like most adults, most of my learning has come through struggle and failure. Of course, the joy of working with community leaders and the impact we've had outweighs all the pain. But, I'm hoping that hearing stories of failure and triumph about me and other Latinas who are fighting on the front lines of change will encourage you. I hope they will help you see that you are not alone.

We need you to be seen and heard. In her masterpiece novel, *The Valley of Amazement*, Amy Tan describes how a servant can be present but treated as though she were invisible: "She had mastered the ever-smiling face of a woman who understood nothing and thus was invisible among them."[5] A lot of what you do might seem invisible or unimportant.

It isn't.

It's essential.

The work you do will be worth it in the end.

Remember, mi hermana, I see you.

Can you see you?

PA' LANTE,
Denise

1

MOVING FROM SURRENDERING
TO THRIVING

Nanci Palacios is the most courageous person in most rooms into which she walks. She is a community organizer who herself is a DACA recipient (an Obama executive order entitled Deferred Action for Childhood Arrivals). DACA allows for young people who came to this country as children to apply for work permits. This has made it possible for Nanci to get a driver's license (unlike in many states, in Florida you cannot have a driver's license if you're not a US citizen) and get a work permit so she can hold a regular job.

Nanci has battled many opponents throughout the years. Every day, when she leaves the house, she's not sure whether that night, her mom and dad will arrive back home. They are both undocumented and have lived in the US for many years. Although they are not allowed to have driver's licenses in Florida, they still need to get to work and pay the bills. So, each day Nanci walks out the door and kisses her mom and dad goodbye, wondering if it is the last time she will see them.

Nanci attended a briefing for donors in New York City, hosted by a generous supporter who had a large, spacious home in Midtown Manhattan. She wore a flowery dress, a sharp pair of heels, and glasses that kept sliding down her nose. Although she was the most courageous person in the room, no one saw it. She yielded to the leadership of the men in the room, who had less experience and less direct knowledge of the issue that undocumented families deal with every day. Before the event started, she was glued to her laptop. During the presentation, she gave her power up to the other people in the room. Actually, she handed it over on a silver platter. She was uncomfortable in the setting, and it showed. In that space, Nanci was not thriving.

Several months later, I visited the home of an undocumented woman with Nanci. The woman was afraid and intimidated by the current administration's dragnet of immigration raids throughout the country. In that setting, sitting across the kitchen table, Nanci's love, inspiration, and determination captivated us. She shared a detailed analysis of the ways that local governments in Florida were cooperating with immigration enforcement agents. She told her personal story in a deep and compelling way. Her passion and knowledge motivated everyone in the room to take action.

Later that year, I attended a regional training in Dallas. Nanci showed up with jeans, sassy shoes, leather jacket, and bright lipstick. Her lashes and brows were on fleek. She was providing powerful testimony in front of a room filled with faith and community leaders from Texas, Alabama, and Florida. She was on fire! She stood up front in her full light and shared her story of the battles she has fought with her people. She told us about how she walked one hundred miles between Orlando and Tampa on a pilgrimage for immigration reform, showed up at every event her local congressman attended—even met his wife to get the message through. She fought to hold a local prosecutor accountable for his inhumane positions on immigration and his harsh punishment of Black people in his prosecution and sentencing choices.

That cold day in Dallas, Nanci laid out a plan to send a message to her local sheriff and sheriffs around the country, that making money by breaking up immigrant families and criminalizing Black folks is immoral and will become politically unpopular. She wasn't wishing for a new reality to come along. She wasn't wondering where her limits were, she was stretching herself past her limits. Finally, she wasn't waiting for permission or answers to come from others. She was designing strategy herself, with community leaders and pastors at her side. She had pushed past her fear and intimidation. She proposed running offense against one of the architects of her misery and the misery of her people.

She finished by saying, "This administration thinks I'm a threat. And now that I think of it, they're right. I am a threat. So they'd better watch out!" To that, faith leaders from three states filled the hall with applause, shouts, and table pounding.

I saw Nanci in Florida one day after the Supreme Court of the United States decided to let the Deferred Action for Childhood Arrivals (DACA) executive order stand. She hadn't slept much the night before because she and others had been celebrating the victory. She was at a Juneteenth rally and protest. She looked giddy, happy-tired, and powerful!

Nanci keeps throwing victories up on the board. Yet, she's going beyond winning in the fight for change—she's thriving. She's taking the fight to her opponents by walking in the fullest, most brilliant version of herself today and for our future.

What Does Thriving Look Like?

Nanci's story shows how she is growing into her leadership and thriving in the fight. There are three keys to thriving in the fight for social change: *lead, live,* and *love.* There are also three surefire signs to warn you when you start surrendering in the fight: *wish, wonder,* and *wait.*

Thriving in the fight means being active, being engaged, and passionately contributing to bringing about needed social, economic, and political change. The opposite of staying in the fight is surrendering, giving up, or passively standing by while problems get worse.

You are thriving in the fight when you are bringing your fullest, sharpest thinking to the day's most pressing problems. You are most likely to do this when you are rested and have created routines that give you enough space to think. Leaders who are thriving in the fight are grounded in their love and passionate commitment to people, family, and justice. This love and passion fuels entire movements. When you are tied in to your love, your anger at injustice serves as a crystalizing agent for your thinking. It can help you forge a path forward that no one can see but you.

When you're thriving, you're leading with your full heart, soul, and mind and your leadership is growing. You are committed to always learning. You lead with confidence, charisma, and courage. You stand up tall, you enter places you know are yours to own, and people can almost see the warmth and glow of your joy and power. When you laugh, you laugh with all of you. You show others the full truth of who you are as a person, and you encourage others to reciprocate. You show up in multiracial spaces as the most open, resilient version of you. You handle stressful situations with grace. You're thriving in the fight when you're successfully integrating your work and your personal life, not compartmentalizing. You build strong relationships and develop strong leaders. Leaders who are thriving in the fight are making steady progress on issues that are important to your Tía Carmen.

I'm inviting you to help create organizations that are willing to listen to you, center your leadership, and be loyal to you when you go through hard times.

Black women, Latinas, and all women of color are the backbone of the social change movement. Since the work you do as a change agent is important, we need you thriving in the fight for change.

You do consequential work. You confront immigration systems that demean your families, schools that can't see the possibility in your children, police violence and gun violence that continues unabated because of a lack of political will, and public health care systems woefully unprepared to protect children and their families from illness. These realities are cosigned by unaccountable government officials and a democracy that is being tested on a daily basis. Hermana, you stand toe-to-toe against corporate giants, political leaders, and widely accepted public opinion that is eventually proven wrong. You believe the world is round, while others still worry about falling off its edge.

Let's be clear. It's not just on those of us who identify as women of color to stay in the fight, change the internal organizational systems, *and* battle the injustices facing our world. Creating change is on all of us.

We need people and institutions to be committed to your long-term development, not just using you up until you have nothing more to give and then throwing you away. Some organizational leaders have no idea how to set you up for success. This must stop.

The same applies to our country. When we create a country where Black and Brown bodies truly thrive, everyone will thrive. Our descendants deserve nothing less from us.

Former US surgeon general Vivek Murthy was asked to name the leading disease affecting Americans. His response: "It's not cancer, it's not heart disease. It's isolation."[1] The COVID-19 epidemic required people to wear masks and physically distance from one another. Yet, Nanci and other sisters like her found ways to strengthen ties between people regardless of the limits placed around them.

Our country needs you. As the pandemic swept through the United States, elected officials made faulty decisions that cost lives. Many of the people who got ill, were hospitalized, and died from the illness were disproportionately Black, Latino, and

Native American. While officials fumbled the ball, women-of-color organizers around the country pivoted all their work to online organizing, delivering food, money, and masks to people in the poorest communities. Women in communities of color rose up to protect the hardest-to-reach families and helped them stay safe.

Three Keys to Thriving in the Fight: Lead, Live, and Love

I have identified three keys to thriving in the fight for social change. They are lead, live, and love. (See figure 3.)

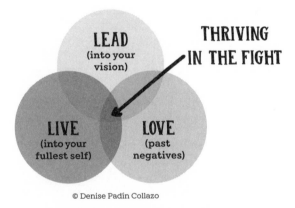

© Denise Padín Collazo

FIGURE 3. Three keys to thriving in the fight

In Spanish there is a saying, "Adelante todo el tiempo, pa' traz ni pa' coger impulso." It means "Always forward, never backward, not even to gather momentum."

I'm inviting you to lead into

➼ your values

➼ your dreams of a better future

➤ your beliefs that, together, people can change the world

➤ your hope that your work can make the world a better place for future generations

➤ your faith in a future that has not yet been seen

I'm inviting you to live into the fullest version of you to

➤ Reject those messages ingrained in you by faith, family, culture, and experience that tell you to just keep your head down and do the work.

➤ Take off your cape and stop trying to be a superhero.

➤ Care for your needs too, not just the needs of everyone else.

➤ Reject limits that you or others have placed on you.

➤ Lead in ways that are authentic to you.

➤ Speak up, speak out, and lead from the front.

➤ Dream big and believe that you, my sister, are a threat to the status quo.

➤ Do things you're not yet comfortable doing.

➤ Know yourself well enough to show up as the best version of yourself everywhere you go.

I'm also inviting you to love past some negatives. I invite you to love past

➤ the negative forces that make you want to give up

➤ despair, discouragement, and disappointment

➤ opponents who try to intimidate you into standing down

➤ people who tell you that your way is not the "right" way

➤ racism, colonized thinking, and anti-Blackness in you, your culture of origin, and society

We need you to thrive in the fight. In order to change, I'm inviting you to lead into your vision, live into the fullest version of you, and love past negatives that hold you back.

What Does Surrendering Look Like?

> Leaders who have already surrendered the fight are passive. They tread water, follow the rules, and stay busy. Surrendered leaders persevere through exhaustion.

On the opposite end of the spectrum from thriving in the fight is surrendering in the fight. Surrender means giving up, or passively standing by while problems get worse. Leaders who have already surrendered the fight are passive. They tread water, follow the rules, and stay busy. Surrendered leaders persevere through exhaustion.

We have likely all experienced surrender at some point or other. Perhaps you haven't even realized it. There's no judgment here. This book is an invitation for you to move into your fullest leadership.

Three Warning Signs of Surrendering in the Fight: Wish, Wonder, and Wait

Three signs that you may be surrendering in the fight are when you find yourself wishing, wondering, and waiting (see figure 4).

Surrender wishes for a new future but isn't sure how to make it happen. Surrendered leaders stay working in settings in which they are most comfortable. Surrender works insane hours, travels too much, and holds these sacrifices up as badges of honor.

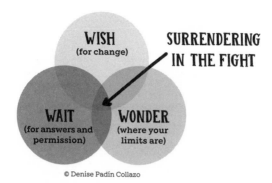

© Denise Padín Collazo

FIGURE 4. Three warning signs of surrendering in the fight

Surrender wonders what could have been. Surrender wonders what happens outside the limits of their comfort zone and accepts personal limitations (imposed by self or others). Leaders who have surrendered in the fight often put their heads down and do the work.

Surrender waits for solutions and implementation plans to arrive. Surrendered leaders wait for permission and approval. Leaders who have surrendered may still technically be in the fight, but they've given up and are checked out.

When you are able to move out of surrender and toward thriving, you can have a greater impact. You can continue to stand strong with and for your communities. And you will find yourself leading more creatively and making better decisions.

The Spectrum from Surrendering to Thriving

I mentioned earlier that one of the symptoms of white supremacy is binary thinking. As such, I have created this value model (see table 1) that you can use to assess your own leadership. The first column describes the status of your leadership on a spectrum from surrendering to thriving. The second column gives examples of how you act at each level of leadership. The third column shows how you may increase your impact as you move from one stage of your leadership to the next. Take a moment to review the chart below with your own leadership in mind.

TABLE 1. The spectrum between surrendering and thriving

STATUS	HOW YOU ACT	YOUR IMPACT
Thriving in the fight	**Fully** integrating chosen family and work **Comfortably** leading from the front **Consistently and strategically** disrupting anti-Blackness **Crystal clear** about your purpose **Successfully** resourcing your work and helping others do the same	x 10
Winning in the fight	**Consistently** integrating chosen family and work **Leading** from the front **Consistently** disrupting anti-Blackness **Leading** with purpose **Successfully** resourcing your own work	x 5
Staying in the fight	**Occasionally** integrating chosen family and work **Leading** from the back **Occasionally** disrupting anti-Blackness **Implementing** someone else's purpose **Partially** resourcing your own work	x 4
Surviving in the fight	**Compartmentalizing** chosen family and work **Leading** from behind the scenes **Noticing and naming** anti-Blackness **Leading** wherever you are needed **Struggling** to resource your work	x 2
Surrendering in the fight	**Sacrificing** chosen family for work **Following** the lead of others who know less than you about your community **Pretending** anti-Blackness doesn't exist **Following** the rules set out by others **Depending** on others to resource your work	x 1

Now that you've reviewed the spectrum from surrendering to thriving with your leadership in mind, note where you see your leadership today (surrendering, surviving, staying, winning, thriving, or add a new category). Write your response in a notebook, make a voice recording, or use the following space.

Okay, now, note where you'd like to see your leadership in three months and why (surrendering, surviving, staying, winning, thriving, or add a new category).

Finally, lay out one step you could take to grow your leadership. Here are some ideas to get your juices flowing:

- Read an article or book on anti-Blackness.
- Ask your manager to help you grow in one area.
- Accept an invitation to lead publicly.
- Take a step to raise money.
- Identify a mentor to help you grow in one area.
- Say *no* to a work event so you can say *yes* to a chosen family activity.

Now it's your turn. Note one step you will take to grow your leadership.

_____

_____

_____

I'd encourage you to share this one-step intention to change with someone you trust. Ideally, it is a person who can help hold you accountable to your desire. You can even set a time on your calendar now to meet with them in three months to share what you've learned. If you have a person in mind, make a note of their name now.

_____

Don't Wish, Wonder, and Wait

At Faith in Action, there was a period of years during which our organization was having difficulty retaining, training, promoting, and centering the leadership and vision of Black women and women of color more broadly. The Black women in our organization came together and partnered with the rest of the Black Caucus to put forth a set of demands of the network. They recommended that the network commission a report on the state of Black women in Faith in Action. Black women were at the center of asking for the report, creating the request for proposals for the report, shaping the questions on the report, and making sure it happened.

The report came up with a number of key recommendations. But as you know, organizational change can be slow. As such, a few women recognized the urgency of implementing one of the report's recommendations right away, to protect from future departures.

Phyllis Hill, Rev. Dr. Cassandra Gould, Rev. Jennifer Jones, Isabelle Moses, Felicia Yoda, Megan Black, and Crystal Cumbo-Montague (the Black Women's Caucus Planning Committee) started to put together a curriculum for the development of Black women organizers that includes over seventy Black women working across the national network in nearly every role across directors, community organizers, and operations staff.

The key insight from the research is that Black women needed intentional development rooted in the incredible lineage of Black women organizers and activists, including Sojourner Truth, Fannie Lou Hamer, and Ella Baker. Phyllis and Dr. Gould led the first session on Womanist Theology, which is a Black-woman-centered approach to theological insight founded by Dr. Katie Cannon. For too long, we've been asked to follow organizing models steeped in patriarchy and whiteness when, instead, we can learn from Black women who have paved the way for us to be where we are today.

Had Phyllis and the Black Women's Caucus taken the stance of wish, wonder, and wait, we might still be waiting for the report's recommendations to be implemented. Had they only wished for a different future, they'd likely still be wishing. Had my sisters wondered where their own limits were, we probably wouldn't have a curriculum completed. Together, they assembled the organizing, theological, and power framework for a tool that signals to Black women in organizing loudly and clearly, "We see you! We love you and we want you here with us." Finally, had they waited for permission for all this to happen, we'd likely still be waiting. They sought the answers to the challenges they were seeing and acted strategically. They looked to themselves and to other experts for the wisdom, and together, they had all the relationships and tools they needed.

(2)

INTEGRATING FAMILY AND WORK

I was wearing a cute pair of heels and my best maternity outfit. Like any good community organizer, I was walking around the packed Oakland Convention Center as the mayor and other officials responded to our vision for the city.

Shortly thereafter, I became the first organizer at Faith in Action (formerly PICO National Network) to give birth, take maternity leave, and then come back to work as an organizer. I was given a generous parental leave of three months twenty-five years ago (which wasn't enough, but even now, most women still have to fight to get that much leave before going back to work after childbirth).

I constantly wrestled with how to be a good mom and a good organizer. Mariana Chow, a wise community leader and San Francisco hardware store owner, told me, "Denise, you can't be perfect at home and perfect at work." That was great advice for a perfectionist and overfunctioner like me.

I negotiated my schedule with my boss to work four long days Monday through Thursday. That way I could take care of Baby Elisa Friday, Saturday, and Sunday. My husband Julio Cesar took care of her two days a week and the other two days she was with her Aita (Elisa's nickname for her Abuela Carmen—my Mom).

Later, when I became the executive director of Faith in Action Bay Area (formerly San Francisco Organizing Project), my board approved my request to work three-quarters time. That made it more possible for me to manage the work, the commute, and my family responsibilities. It was the weirdest feeling to be the executive director and get up and leave the office (while other staff were still working) so I could pick up Elisa from elementary school after care, and start the long commute home. My board and staff supported the accommodation, which made it possible to continue in that top leadership role.

> **At the end of my life, I don't think I'll wish I had spent more time on conference calls or pulling weeds. I will, though, probably wish I had spent more time stacking rocks.**

Some days, I'd look up and realize it was time to go. I had been running around in meetings or calls all day and hadn't peed or eaten for hours. Still, the mountain of work in front of me could have landed me into the next month.

Once I picked Elisa up from elementary school after care, while sitting in traffic, I would think, "Might as well return a few calls." By the time I got home, a few had turned into ten. Before kicking off my heels I'd start with dinner and cleanup. Some nights, I'd sneak out to the supermarket, talk to my prima on the phone, and walk slowly down the lonely aisles behind an autopiloted grocery cart.

When she was three years old, my grandbaby Leyla Rose and I were sitting outside at Aita's house. Leyla was purposefully stacking rocks. I was sitting on the ground with her in the morning sun. I kept noticing mini-weeds sprouting up through the rocks. I thought to myself, "I could weed this whole area for my Mom while Leyla plays." Then I caught myself and wondered, "Why must I always feel like I have to produce?" I steadied myself, breathed, and redirected my energy to helping construct Leyla's rock palace.

At the end of my life, I don't think I'll wish I had spent more time on conference calls or pulling weeds. I will, though, probably wish I had spent more time stacking rocks.

Women of Color Produce

These glimpses into my life highlight the ways that women of color produce. We all have experience with current family members or ancestors who were paid for their work by the piece. Your abuela might have picked peaches, harvested oranges, or like my Abuela Lela, sewn garments and assembled custom jewelry by the piece. Our Native and African ancestors whose work was stolen through slavery produced the wealth of nations. The Hebrew scriptures describe slaves who successfully made bricks without straw. In organizational settings and in personal settings, we usually carry outsized responsibilities, usually without the commensurate resources, recognition, or room for reflection to succeed. We get the job done, often at tremendous cost to our psyches, bodies, families, and careers.

While some of our dilemma has to do with organizational cultures, part of the challenge is internal to us. In our families and in our worlds, when things go wrong, we tend to be the first people to grab a mop. While this is a great instinct when your kid spills milk at the dinner table, it's not a great strategy for thriving.

Work–Life Balance? or Family Work Integration?

Dr. Stacy Blake-Beard is a visiting professor at Dartmouth College's Tuck School of Business. I met Dr. Blake-Beard several years back when she taught as part of Women and Power, an Executive Education course I attended at the Harvard Kennedy School of Government. Stacy has had a profound impact on my thinking about the issue of "work-life balance." She has conducted extensive research on women's mentorship. Her research into the emerging role of women in the workplace in India uncovered a simple truth. When you ask women about their responsibilities at home and at work, they usually start by talking about family. Family comes first, work second. I've followed her lead in using the language "family-work integration" instead of "work-life balance" for this reason. When we use the word "family," there is a built-in assumption that this applies to the family who are linked to you by choice and by blood. I've also chosen to place this chapter early in the book to recognize the importance that family plays in our lives, especially as Latinas.

Dr. Blake-Beard helped me with an off-the-cuff observation: "The only time you're balanced is when you're dead." That's true. I've found the Family Work Integration concept more helpful than seeking the unattainable "work-life balance." First, because it starts with family; second, it focuses on integration and not compartmentalization. My colleagues often ask me how to be a change agent *and* live a whole, fulfilling life outside of work. That, mi hermana, is one of the biggest questions we must answer.

Culture of Urgency

In addition to the fact that women carry outsized caregiving and family responsibilities, another reason it's hard to thrive in the fight for change is because it seems like everything we face is urgent. This "culture of urgency" is a symptom of white supremacy that exists in our system, our institutions, and us regardless of our own racial identity. In *Dismantling Racism: A Workbook for*

Social Change Groups, Tema Okun and other authors define the full list of white supremacy characteristics as

> perfectionism, a sense of urgency, defensiveness, valuing quantity over quality, worship of the written word, belief in only one right way, paternalism, either/or thinking, power hoarding, fear of open conflict, individualism, belief that I'm the only one (who can do this "right"), the belief that progress is bigger and more, a belief in objectivity, and claiming a right to comfort[1]

They describe a sense of urgency as follows:

- continued sense of urgency that makes it difficult to take time to be inclusive, encourage democratic and/or thoughtful decision-making, to think long-term, to consider consequences
- frequently results in sacrificing potential allies for quick or highly visible results, for example sacrificing interests of communities of color in order to win victories for white people (seen as default or norm community)
- reinforced by funding proposals which promise too much work for too little money and by funders who expect too much for too little

Sound familiar?

Until we come up with better answers for how to integrate family and work and how to defeat the culture of urgency in our movement, we will continue to lose bold, courageous, visionary leaders because the pace of the work is unsustainable.

Don't Throw Each Other Away

In many change organizations such as political campaigns, canvassing efforts, nonprofit organizations, and movement spaces, women and people of color are treated as dispensable—"use them up until they have finished their purpose and let 'em go." Mijente, an organization led by Marisa Franco and many others, is dedicated to building the political power of the Latinx community. Because people of color are set up to compete with one another in systems, Mijente challenges the tactics of white supremacy by intentionally creating space for principled conflict. Their community is held together by seven agreed-upon principles. Principle 6 is "Don't throw each other away." Here is some of how this principle is described:

> Conflict is inevitable and necessary for honest discourse and unity across differences. We believe building a space that can hold disagreement can lead to greater accountability, resilience and antifragility. This means we won't condone call-outs and exiling each other, or playing oppression olympics with each other. But this also means we don't allow things to fester inside. The state has often robbed us of our ability to transform conflict and hold relationships with one another. Thus we believe principled struggle is central to our capacity to self-govern and build for the long haul.[2]

Thankfully a number of movement spaces like Mijente are emerging that are structured to reinforce healthier ways of operating.

Cycling Women Through

To illustrate how many women get cycled through our organizations, I'll use Faith in Action Network as an example. Over a six-year period between 2011 and 2017, 212 women of color were hired. Over the same period of time 296 women of color left Faith in Action or one of its member federations. The network had done a good job hiring women of color, but a terrible job retaining them.

From what I've seen, this is happening in many justice organizations. Yet, there have been few efforts to seriously track and measure organizations' ability to retain the best and the brightest talent.

We say we measure what we care about. But very few organizations have decided to track this data. Shout-out to Faith in Action for tracking the data and working to develop active strategies to center the leadership of women of color.

When turnover is high, especially among women of color, justice organizations need to ask themselves why. Faith in Action and its member federations lost immeasurable wisdom and knowledge during that six-year period when 296 women of color left. The cost of losing this talent is incalculable.

Family Work Integration as a Tool for Retention

Since then, because of the leadership of Black women in our network, we made many strides forward. In 2017, while serving as chief of staff at Faith in Action, I spearheaded an experiment to provide women of color, and all staff, the important resource of time for reflection, rest, and creativity. We call it the Family Work Integration program. It is a simple, yet powerful, tool to retain, support, and center the leadership of women of color in our workplace.

Here's how the Family Work Integration plan works. Monday through Thursday, all staff are focused on executing their work. Fridays, we've made a commitment to no emails, no meetings or calls. Yes, you read that right. Friday is a paid work day, but our offices close, and people put an out-of-office message on their emails and focus on their own self-directed learning. Here is a sample of the out-of-office message that was developed by our National Staff Coordinating Team (shout-out to Annee Bell,

Felicia Yoda, Monica Sommerville, Joseph Fleming, Mary Obaka, Richard Morales, Risa Brown, and Azim Malikzada, who led the charge on implementing this culture shift, tracking and presenting the data).

If you send an email to a member of the Faith in Action national staff on a Friday, you might receive this out-of-message reply from them (see figure 5).

> Thanks for your email.
>
> Faith in Action believes in the potential for the transformation of people, institutions, and our larger culture. In an effort to continue transforming the communities in which we live, Faith in Action National has designated each Friday as a day to allow staff to unleash their creativity, develop themselves personally and professionally, and preserve their health. Our offices are closed on Fridays; we will resume normal business hours on Monday.

© Faith in Action

FIGURE 5. Family Work Integration out-of-office email reply

The program was built on the following three concepts.

Structural Change to Focus on Getting Better

In a TED Talk, Eduardo Briceño describes how Beyoncé, arguably one of the most successful entertainers of our time, has created intentional structures to get better.[3] After each show, she reviews the video of the show and makes detailed notes for her dancers, production crew, and so on. She is committed to improving, despite being one of the best in the industry. The Family Work Integration plan created a simple, structural change to help staff get better at their work. So often, people in the nonprofit sector are overworked and under-resourced in their roles. Our intention was to create a structural change that allowed space for growth. By clearly stating that 20 percent of staff time was being set aside for them to focus on their development, their creativity, and getting better at their work, the organization was sending a clear message.

If you were a concert pianist, you would never imagine performing more than you practiced. Yet in the fight for social change sometimes we perform 110 percent of the time, and leave little room for practice and intentional growth. This program is designed to create a new reality for employees.

Targeted Universalist Approach

The second concept that undergirds the Family Work Integration plan is targeted universalism. Targeted universalism means that while it is designed to meet the needs of a specific group of women (Black and Brown women who carry outsized caregiving responsibilities), its benefits accrue to everyone. Targeted universalism is based on the research of Dr. john a. powell (who does not capitalize his name). He leads the Center for Inclusion and Belonging at the University of California, Berkeley. At a July 2015 staff retreat, the Faith in Action national staff team overwhelmingly named the culture of urgency as one of three top cultural roots that were holding us back. The pace of the work in our organization was leading to exhaustion. In consultation with many others, I put forth a plan for taking one step toward addressing the needs of employees who are often the most marginalized in the workplace (Black women) by giving people a release valve each week. The easy way to think about targeted universalism is to think of the curb cuts in sidewalks. The curb cuts in the sidewalk are made for people with limited mobility, but everyone can use them: skateboarders, parents pushing strollers, runners, pedestrians, and so on. The Family Work Integration plan was fashioned with the specific needs of caregivers in mind (that's the targeted part). It also benefits everyone on staff (that's the universalist part).

Promising Data

The work of social change is hard, tiring, and often frenzied work. Family Work Integration encourages people to invest time in their own creativity, growth, and learning. It is about healing, resting, and refilling reserves that fuel creativity. As part of this experiment, we administered a pre- , midpoint- , and post-survey. Here is a chart showing the increases in satisfaction levels (on a scale of 1–10) of our national staff between the pre-test and the post-test during the first year of this experiment. (See figure 6.) To read the chart, start with the first column. To the question "I am satisfied with the quality and time I invest in my professional learning and development," you will see that before Family Work Integration, the weighted average answer of all staff was 5.16 (on a scale of 1–10). At the end of the one-year experiment, the weighted average answer (on a scale of 1–10) went up to 7.12.

If you review the third question about continuing at the current pace, we were surprised to see such marked improvements in people's comfort with the pace of the work in such a short period of time (from 5.6 to 7.5). This improvement in people's perception of the pace of the work could be a way to measure whether or not the organization is effectively tackling the pervasive culture of urgency that plagues the movement for change. We also didn't expect to see improvements in areas such as spiritual growth and balance of activities in life. Figure 7 shows a list of the answers for all questions in the survey. The survey we used was adapted from a document created by the Rockwood Leadership Institute.

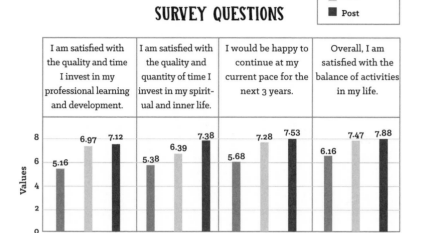

FIGURE 6. Family Work Integration: average weighted scores for key survey questions

Figure 7 shows percentage increase between the first survey and the final survey (conducted one year later). For the third question, "I would be happy to continue at my current pace for the next 3 years," staff reported a 32 percent increase in their agreement with that statement. This is a significant change in perceptions in just one year's time. Of course more research needs to be done to learn more, but the initial results are promising.

We did not expect to see such dramatic changes in responses in just one year, especially given the fact that not everyone participated fully. Some people still have trouble creating the boundaries with themselves or still had workloads that were too heavy to implement this change, especially at the senior staff level. We are coupling this program with assessing the workload for each employee to make sure people can equitably access the program.

SURVEY QUESTIONS

FIGURE 7. Family Work Integration: percentage change from pre-test to post-test survey

© Faith in Action

Survey Question	%
I am satisfied with the quality and time I invest in my professional learning and development.	37.98%
I am satisfied with the quality and quantity of time I invest in my spiritual and inner life.	37.17 %
I would be happy to continue at my current pace for the next 3 years.	32.57%
Overall, I am satisfied with the balance of activities in my life.	27.92%
I invest the quality and quantity of time I would like with my partner.	27.92%
Overall, I invest the needed time and attention to care for the health needs of my body.	27.61%
Overall, my diet is healthy and nutritious.	27.00%
I am satisfied with the quality and quantity of time I invest in my recreational activities.	26.21%
I am satisfied with the quality and quantity of time I invest in my friendships.	25.88%
I take the time and space to stay in touch with and tend to my emotions.	24.34%
I take the amount and variety of exercise needed for good health and sustained energy.	24.23%
I am satisfied with the quality and quantity of time I invest in other aspects of community.	20.82%
Overall, I am satisfied with the way I actually spend my time at work.	20.58%
I wake up in the morning ready to meet life with positive energy.	18.06%
I end my days with a feeling of satisfaction.	14.56%
I get sufficient sleep and rest to sustain my energy.	14.54%
Overall, I am leading the life I would like to lead.	10.19%
I am doing work that is a good expression of my life purpose.	5.52%

Legend: 5.5%, 10.2%, 14.5%, 14.6%, 18.1%, 20.6%, 20.8%, 24.2%, 24.3%, 25.9%, 26.2%, 27.0%, 27.6%, 27.9%, 32.6%, 37.2%, 38%

This is the kind of innovation that can interrupt old, unhealthy patterns in our movement. The results far exceeded our expectations for an intervention that was simple and within our control.

Since we implemented this experiment, three other national organizations and one regional organization have adopted the change. Of course, this is not the only way to combat the culture of urgency that limits our creativity, but it's one that seems to be showing good results so far.

The previous examples include some of the steps I've taken to stay sharp in the fight for social change, raise a family, tend to a personal life, and grow as a human being outside of work. This will look different for each of us.

Applying the Thriving (Lead, Live, Love) and Surrendering (Wish, Wonder, Wait) Framework

Now, let's return to the three keys to *thriving* in the fight (lead, live, love) and three signs of *surrendering* the fight (wish, wonder, wait).

Here is how I integrated the ideas of leading, living, and loving as ingredients for success:

1. **Leading into vision.** I had a vision in my head that it was possible to do the work of community organizing *and* have a family. When I did my research and interviews of the various organizing networks to decide which one to join, I chose Faith in Action (PICO at the time) because it appeared to have a more family-friendly orientation. Then, through my personal experience, I helped to make it so.

2. **Living into the fullest version of myself.** Despite the high points and low points in both my personal life and

my career, I had to dig deep to become the fullest expression of myself. Sometimes I would lead, but not live, into my fullest, generous, loving self. I am learning how to identify and seek out the conditions I need in order to be able to be kind and generous to myself, so I can show love to others. I recognized that always sprinting did not give me the space and time to reflect and recharge. Having that room for reflection helps me show up as more resilient and better able to face challenging situations effectively.

3. **Loving past negatives.** When I was implementing the Family Work Integration plan at Faith in Action, I had to push against skepticism at all levels. There were questions about whether this was needed, whether it would work, and whether we could get people to buy in. Community organizers are incredible justice fighters known for their addiction to urgency and busy-ness, plus they view the world from an antiestablishment bent. Getting them to agree to any one thing is a challenge. I knew that getting them to agree to test this would take work. Yet, I knew from my experience that this effort would benefit so many families. My love for them outweighed the negatives that lay in my path.

Upon reflection, here's how I resisted the three signs of surrendering the fight.

1. **Wishing things were different.** The people who had been successful in my organization before me had a very different vision about what it looked like to have both a family and work. Had I yielded to their vision, my life would look very different than it does now. Had I stopped at wishing for something different, instead of

leading and acting into my vision, perhaps I would have allowed others' opinions to determine my timeline for starting a family, leading as a woman, and so on. Dear One, I've spoken to so many change agents who put off their desire for a family because they were too busy in the work, then later shared their deep lament for the family that never came to be.

> **Dear One, I've spoken to so many change agents who put off their desire for a family because they were too busy in the work, then later shared their deep lament for the family that never came to be.**

2. **Wondering if I could shape culture in this way.** It took me several years to get up the courage to put this idea forward full force. I planted seeds along the way, and tested the idea. But it took a leap of faith in my ability to negotiate this change, get people on board, etc. It also required me to use leverage to get the plan implemented. And at first, I wasn't sure if it would fly.

3. **Waiting for solutions to arrive**. Year after year, I'd watch as Latinas and other women of color would leave the organizing work despite efforts to stem the tide. Those of us in leadership could see the problem. Yet change didn't happen. Finally, I decided to use my relative power and privilege in the network to put forth an innovative solution that was really simple and based in my own personal experience.

Take a Beat to Reflect

Now, may I ask you to pause for a moment?

Imagine what you might do if you had one day per week of unscheduled time that you could invest in your own creativity and development. (Write down some of your ideas in the following space or in a notebook, or make a voice recording of your ideas.)

_____

_____

_____

I know, it can seem overwhelming when you think about all that you're carrying. It felt strange for us at Faith in Action when we began to consider implementing this. After we began the program we started to hear people on our national staff describe how intentionally investing in their own leadership and pushing against the culture of urgency (and martyrdom) has benefitted their lives.

One person described to me how having that day of unscheduled time when at least people inside Faith in Action are limiting email traffic and meetings allows for quiet, uninterrupted time to get caught up on projects. Others take yoga or swim regularly. People care for aging parents or have time to fight with their insurance company. Sometimes the time gets used for planning, reading, and writing. Even getting caught up on sleep!

One member of our staff turned down a much higher-paying job with more prestige because they valued the Family Work Integration benefit more highly than going to work for more pay.

Imagine what could shift for you.

Imagine how a change like this could benefit your organization, your work.

Our opponents are well organized and have lots of money on their side. Could investing in growing our collective creativity as a movement tip the scales ever so slightly on behalf of our families?

We all say we're too busy to stop and think, to rest, recover, reflect, and improve. We all know instinctively this pace is not good for us. It's not good for our long-term health. It's taking years off of our lives.

Your bodies and minds need space to reflect, restore, recharge. Yet caring for yourself is usually your very last priority.

TAKING ACTION

The Family Work Integration plan is a scalable step that organizations can take to challenge the culture of urgency. We invite you to join us in taking your organization through a three-month trial of the Family Work Integration plan.

➡ For help and materials to support you as you implement this experiment, click "Try this on" to download our Toolkit at *DeniseCollazo.com*.

➡ If you would like more information about the program that you can share with your organization, click "Tell me more" at *DeniseCollazo.com*.

A Story of Repairing Hurts

Recently, I took an extended sabbatical to rest, reflect, and recharge for the road ahead. When I get too busy and too overburdened, I tend to have a short temper and very little filter for my words. Since my sabbatical I have been learning how to show up as a fuller version of myself. My colleague Daniel Schwartz, director of Faith in Action Alabama, has been a dedicated community organizer for many years. Sadly, he is one of the people I've harmed along the way. In a conversation that he and I were having to reconcile and start anew, he told me this: "Denise, when you show your love, it is remarkable, not just among organizers, but among human beings." For someone who I've hurt so deeply to tell me something like this was so humbling. He helped me see how much more powerful I am when I lead with my joy and love. When I take off my boxing gloves and show up as my full, loving, caring, self without wondering whether people will like me, they actually like me better. Imagine that. While I'm working to make the world a better place, I'm also hoping to make it a better place for the people closest to me.

I invite you to make the decision to first care for you and yours, so you can more effectively care for others.

3

LEADING FROM THE FRONT

I was in a hotel room in Atlanta when I got the news that I didn't get the job.

I called my best friend Andrea and had a good, hard cry. Julio Cesar, my husband of twenty-five-plus years, calmly wrapped his long arms around me while I spoke to my closest comadre.

It was a tough decision to apply for the national directorship of Faith in Action. At first I decided against applying. In my heart, I knew I probably wouldn't get the job. I felt afraid. I thought, "What if I apply and don't get the job?" I thought of how embarrassing that would be. A very public failure.

Then I decided to apply. Throughout the process I moved from fear, to excitement, to doubt. It was a roller coaster of emotions. There were a number of other applicants from throughout the organization, so for a time, the transition shaped much of our day-to-day work dynamics.

In order to apply for this big national position, I had to stretch myself to and beyond my limits. It tested my writing ability. It tested my relationships. It tested my ability to speak in public. It tested my confidence.

Today I can say that not getting that job was the best thing that ever happened to me. Even though it was what I wanted, it was not what God had planned for me. Applying for the position, not getting it, then staring down my gifts and my gaps was an important experience.

I received valuable, real-time feedback on my leadership. In addition, I developed a more complete topographical map of my environment than I had before. Most importantly, I had followed my own advice.

So many times along the way, women I had worked with had faced a choice point in their lives. Sometimes they would decide not to apply for a position if someone they knew was also applying. Sometimes they would receive invitations to consider big promotions but would take themselves out of the running, saying, "I'm not ready." I decided there was no way I could authentically encourage women to make big bets on themselves if I didn't do it myself.

> **Trying to lead from the front and failing broke my heart. But it broke my heart *open*.**

Trying to lead from the front and failing broke my heart. But it broke my heart *open*. I realized the ways I had been showing up as only part of myself to others. I had been so extremely hard on myself, and expecting perfection, that I had allowed that to bleed out to others. My inability to accept myself as who I was made it hard for me to accept people around me for who they were and what they brought.

My colleague Felicia Yoda once said to me, "Denise, in what world do you wake up each day and not make mistakes?" I responded, "In the world I've made up in my head." She and many others showed me, through their love, warmth, and support, how to love and accept myself, so that I could extend that love outward to a broader circle of people. I had been reserving my love only for those closest to me. I had been stingy about showing my heart, concern, and love to those who were further out.

Rev. Alvin Herring was chosen to serve as the national executive director of Faith in Action. He has been a blessing to me and to the network. He has treated me with nothing but compassion, love, and respect. He sees me. He gave me direct, honest feedback about the way people had been experiencing me. He approved my request for a sabbatical break so I could rest, reflect, and recharge for the road ahead. Together, we have walked carefully on a journey that has shifted my outlook, improved my relationships with family and colleagues, and resulted in an exponential increase in my joy and impact. I consider him both a mentor and a friend and feel tremendously grateful for his investment in me and my leadership.

That night in Atlanta, I tasted defeat. Now, I see that I had taken a wonderful chance to stretch myself, and I allowed people to love me past the things that were holding me back. It didn't turn out how I had imagined. Yet, I wouldn't trade the outcome for the world. I'm leading from the front in different ways. I've served as a national movement leader in Latinx and multiracial spaces; I've had the opportunity to share the message of this book with thousands of people around the globe. I have found myself feeling joyful in my role more days than not. And sister, since there are so few Latinas and women of color in the movement, we need you leading joyfully from the front too.

There Are Too Few Latinas Leading from the Front

Currently, one in five women in the US are Latina. By 2060, nearly one out of every three women in America will be Latina.[1] Yet despite the growing demographic, Latinas are underrepresented at every level of leadership.

Every time I speak in public I learn that Latinas and other women of color are dying to hear my voice, a voice like theirs. When I tell them I'm writing a book, they tell me to hurry up and finish it! I walk into too many spaces that are national or international in scope, and the voices of Latinas are muted. When I sit in boardrooms that are all male, other women like my colleague Lise Afoy walk by, smile, and silently mouth the words "girl power" to me. Our wisdom and vision are missing in too many spaces. As we understand the conditions we need to succeed, and create them for ourselves, we grow exponentially.

Based on my personal experience and that of many others, Latinas and women of color more broadly are held back in the movement for social change in the following ways.

Few Promotions to Top Leadership Positions

Without key interventions by individuals and organizations, the patterns that have plagued the social change movement for the last quarter century will continue. Many Black and Brown women are hired into the work but are not ascending to the highest leadership positions. Often, the waiting time for a founder or a senior leader to transition out of an executive role outlasts women's timeframes. Some Latinxs solve this problem by creating new leadership spaces where they can grow and develop at their own pace.

Insufficient Retention

Many talented Latinas and other women of color leave through the back door. They get hired but don't stay. We need them to stay in the fight. We need to create conditions for them to succeed. Retention of Latinas and other women of color in leadership positions in the fight for social change is a key limiting reagent in the equation for change. It's limiting our progress. A first step to addressing this problem would be to measure this. We measure what we care about.

Limited Public Leadership (and Recognition That Comes with It)

Many Latinas and other women of color are hesitant to lead from the front, timid about asking for what they need to integrate family and work, and reluctant to lead across race. As such, many leaders who have tremendous talent don't progress at the same rate as their male counterparts. If you're always leading from behind the scenes, it's tough for people to see the through line between you and the work that you're doing.

Organizational Failure

Many organizational and movement leaders don't know how to support the leadership of Latinas and lack basic understanding of how to create conditions for them to reach their greatest capacity. Nonprofits need a system for filtering out top leaders who are unable to successfully work across race and culture.

Danger of Re-creating Old Patterns

Latinas are stepping into formal leadership at a greater pace in recent years (elected officials, CEOs, senior and executive leaders in nonprofits). But if we're not careful, as leaders we can re-create old patterns and organizational practices that are rooted in white supremacy (such as the culture of urgency and overwork), which will not result in our collective liberation. For example, it's so easy to fall into the trap in which women of color find themselves competing against each other for organizational crumbs instead of leading the real change that is needed.

There Are Few Formal Structures for Women's Mentorship

In the field of community organizing, we have a principle that says "Structures channel power." This means that when there are no structures in place, it's hard to focus power. Despite having no formal mechanisms or support for doing this, I have made a purposeful effort to invest in the leadership and growth of women around me. Many Black and Brown women do this informally as an add-on to their job. They do not get paid for this additional work, nor is it included in the job responsibilities. They do it anyway. Imagine how impactful it would be if investments were made to support an authentic, affinity-based framework for mentoring women's leadership in the field of social change.

The Hispanic Community Is under Attack

This country needs women more than it ever has before. Today we must slay the dragons that are threatening our families—greedy people who run corporations more focused on making money than paying people what their precious work is truly worth, plus weak politicians who care more about getting reelected than creating flourishing communities where our kids and families can thrive. We are fighting against an entire system that was birthed, bathed, and raised in white supremacy. We ourselves grew up and were raised in schools, congregations, and other community institutions that held a "white is right" approach to the world. It will take all of us using all our energy, creativity, and passion to defeat these evils.

During this moment in our country and our world, Latinx communities are under attack like never before. The starkest example is the 2019 mass shooting in El Paso, Texas, a city located two miles from Ciudad Juarez in the Mexican state of Chihuahua. In the United States, the Latinx population has grown to fifty-nine million and is now the largest minority group.[2] In an April 2019 poll for Univisión, the Latinx-owned polling firm Latino Decisions discovered that 81 percent of registered Latino voters who were polled said they believe that anti-Latinx racism is a growing problem in America.[3] Two months later, in June 2019, that number rose to 86 percent.[4] This survey was taken before the El Paso shooting, which Stuart Anderson of Forbes.com reported as follows:[5]

> On August 3, 2019, a (white) gunman at a Walmart in El Paso, Texas attempted to shoot as many Latinos as possible before surrendering to police. He killed 22 people and injured many more. He told police he targeted Mexican immigrants and had produced a manifesto that declared "This attack is a response to the Hispanic invasion of Texas."

One month after the El Paso shooting, in September 2019, the number of Latino registered voters who believed that anti-Latino racism is a growing problem went up to 87 percent.[6]

Latinas Must Lead from the Front

While Latinos have grown to become the most numerous ethnic minority in the US, there are very few Latinas leading from the front. Because there are so few of us in up-front leadership, we cannot wait for invitations to lead. Instead, Latinx sisters who want to thrive need to *aspire* to lead from the front. When Latinas aren't present in decision-making spaces, the broader movement for change is missing an important perspective from the country's largest ethnic group.

Throughout my career, I've lost track of the number of times I've walked into a large room of senior leaders and counted only a couple of other Latinas. When I attend events, many Latinas sit as close to the back of the room as possible. Or, even worse, my sisters are staring into a computer screen instead of talking to the people around them.

Despite the powerful role that women play in the fabric of our Latino cultures, in public, we often operate behind the scenes. I'm inspired by some of my colleagues and friends who have made the choice to run for office and won: Angela Cobián is a school board member in Denver, Angelica Rubio serves as state senator in New Mexico, Johana Bencomo recently won a city council seat in Las Cruces, New Mexico, and Debbie Ingram serves as a state senator in Vermont. Around the country, women are entering the political world in numbers not seen before. According to the Reflective Democracy Campaign, since 2012, women of color candidates for Congress have increased by 75 percent, but they still represent less than 10 percent of the candidates for Congress overall. White men have eight times more political power than women of color.[7] We have a few more women of color electeds, but women of color are still woefully underrepresented in our country's political leadership.

> **White men have eight times more political power than women of color.**

Like Congress, many of the change-making spaces we navigate were not built for us: foundations, corporate headquarters, halls of government—often our own organizations were not built with us in mind. In addition, each of us may have diverse pictures of what leadership looks like.

Because People See the World in Patterns, We Need to Show Them New Pictures

When people haven't seen examples of something before, they refer back to old patterns of what they have seen. Research by Dr. Iris Bohnet shows this to be true. She uses the following example in a lecture she gives entitled "Seeing Is Believing." When you think of a kindergarten teacher, you usually think of a woman. When people do see a male kindergarten teacher, it is usually a surprise. This is because it breaks the pattern that most people have in their head about the expected gender of a kindergarten teacher. We see leadership in the world in patterns as well.

An example of how people's expectations are informed by the patterns they've experienced happened on the night before the 2018 election, in Las Cruces, New Mexico. Johana Bencomo was canvassing with her mother and grandmother in one of the wealthier parts of her district. "It was the proudest moment in the campaign for me to have my Mom and Abuela with me. As I walked up to the house, a group of gentlemen were painting the house." She asked them in Spanish if the homeowner was there, and they waved her through to the front door. She spoke to the voter and asked for his vote. On the way out, one of the painters asked, "¿Mija, andas buscando casas para limpiar?" Johana explained that no, she wasn't looking for houses to clean, she was running for city council. The men eagerly took literature to share with others. At first, Johana laughed this moment off, wondering if she had dressed up enough that day. Upon further reflection she noted, "While las mujeres who clean houses are real heroes, why wouldn't we imagine something else? My people cannot even dream. It was the most magical, and heartbreaking, moment of my campaign."[8] The next day, she won her race for city council.

As Dr. Bohnet's research shows, when people haven't seen an example of something before (like a young Latina knocking on doors to get elected for city council), they assume she's part of a pattern they *have* seen before (three Latinas in a wealthy neighborhood looking for a house to clean). We need to show people new pictures of what leadership looks like to stretch their imagination.

Moving Past Discomfort

Let's admit, it's often more comfortable to lead from behind the scenes. As Latinas, we have been taught by faith, family, culture, tradition, and experience to serve, be humble, and seek no reward or recognition for our work.

But leading from behind is not enough. We need to come out of the dark. We must be willing to be "seen" and recognized. We need to stop shying away from the spotlight and handing our power to others. Our people expect us to use all of our voice, all of our gifts, all of our power. I have a magnet on my fridge that says "Life begins at the end of your comfort zone." In order to lead in public more effectively, Latinas and all women of color must move past what's comfortable. Research by Dr. Robert Livingston shows that when we're uncomfortable or feeling "low power," we don't negotiate as well as we do when we're feeling confident.

We're also less charismatic when we're uncomfortable. In her book *The Charisma Myth: How Anyone Can Master the Art and Science of Personal Magnetism*, Harvard/MIT lecturer Olivia Fox Cabane writes, "Being charismatic means overcoming mental and physical discomfort. . . . Feeling discomfort, whether physical or mental, can affect your performance and emotions, as well as others' perception of you."[9]

In order to leverage much more leadership in our communities, we must translate the relational and effective leadership of our women into the kind of comfortable, charismatic public leadership that our matriarchs and emerging sisters exercise in our families.

Women like Johana are realizing that if Latinxs are not willing to transition from behind-the-scenes leader to public leader, others will speak for our communities. Also, we need to go beyond just representing our own communities; we need to build bridges to other communities and weave together relationships across cultures and races who also could benefit from our leadership.

We must know our history and be willing to tell our stories in public. We need to stop shrinking, slumping, making ourselves smaller than we are. A popular TED Talk featuring social psychologist and Harvard lecturer Amy Cuddy shows that there is an actual connection between how powerful we feel and how much space we take up.[10] She describes assuming a "power pose" in which you stand up tall and take up as much space as you can before doing something that requires all your power. An even more exciting revelation of her research is that the reverse is also true. In essence, when you stand up taller, you also feel more powerful. We need to have a bigger vision for our own leadership, not just the leadership of others. We need to have a plan for our own career path and development. Jim Rohn, an entrepreneur and motivational speaker, says, "If you don't design your own life plan, chances are you'll fall into someone else's plan. And guess what they have planned for you? Not much."

When I returned to work from sabbatical on May 1, 2019, I set what I thought was a stretch goal of writing twenty articles within one year. Yet, by then, I had hit that goal *and* was almost finished writing this book! The book hadn't initially been on my list of goals. Even when we think we're stretching ourselves, we can still underestimate our capacity and have trouble envisioning a new future reality. Of course, none of us could have predicted the disruption and life-changing impacts that COVID-19 would have on our lives, yet we all managed to carry much more than we could have ever imagined as a global pandemic swept over us.

We need to practice leading in public. We need to be willing to grab the mic and become comfortable, powerful, up-front leaders in our own authentic ways (not in the egocentric ways that repel us). We also need to model how to do this for others.

Examples of Modeling Leadership for Others

Modeling what leadership can look like for others is very important. Like it or not, we are all role models for someone else. People are watching you. When you thrive, you can model healthy leadership for others. Here are some of the ways that I have modeled leadership that I try to actively think about. For example, as I decided to write this book, I have engaged a team of twelve colleagues to serve as the Thriving in the Fight Advisory Board. This has helped them all shape and shepherd the message of the book. At the same time, they have learned a lot in the process. Another simple way to model leadership is when you notice a newer staff member or volunteer who seems to gravitate toward you, make it a point to engage them genuinely. Also, when you observe that a woman of color is doing work that others aren't naturally seeing, shout her out for her work and lift her up in public ways. These are a few examples of how to lead in a way that you are modeling good leadership for others. There are certainly many more possibilities for how to do this; the important thing is to do it. Now, let's return to the thriving and surrendering framework as it applies to leading from the front.

Revisiting the Thriving and Surrendering Framework

To refresh our memories, here is a little cheat sheet (see table 2) to help you remember the three keys to thriving (lead, live, love) and the three signs of surrendering (wish, wonder, wait).

TABLE 2. Thrive and surrender cheat sheet

THREE KEYS TO THRIVING IN THE FIGHT	THREE SIGNS OF SURRENDERING THE FIGHT
Lead into your vision.	**Wish** for a future reality.
Live into your fullest self.	**Wonder** where your limits are.
Love past negatives that hold you back.	**Wait** for permission and answers to come from others.

© Denise Padín Collazo

Lead into Your Vision

Despite the underrepresentation in the formal systems of our democracy and our institutions, our families and communities are leaderful. My Titi Norma leads the heck out of our family. She convenes them over food; she includes people who try to stay on the periphery. She calls every member of our family on their birthday and sings the full "Happy Birthday" song—every year! Yet, if you asked her to speak in front of a roomful of people, she'd rather die.

Live into Your Fullest Self

In order to show up as our fullest selves outside the spaces where we feel safe, we need to consider trying on some new things. We need to let go of some of the old mindsets that have gotten us this far and try on some new things that may not feel comfortable at first. For example, a few years back, I realized that I was feeling terrified every time I was asked to speak or present in front of large groups. One time I walked all the way up on stage to speak, said a few words, then quickly ran back off stage! To conquer this fear, I decided to join Toastmasters to help me grow my public speaking skills. I learned that a big part of being comfortable speaking in public is advance preparation and practice. Now, instead of avoiding public speaking, I am working to improve. As I get better, I learn how to better prepare and get more practice. It's a virtuous cycle. Now, I feel much more comfortable speaking in large groups than I did before. With that simple step, I'm growing into a fuller version of myself.

Love Past Negatives That Hold You Back

Instead of skipping that dreaded pre-event networking dinner, could you figure out how to get there? Even if that means leaving the main event early. When you find yourself in an uncomfortable setting during a lunch break, could you resist the temptation to run for the door to take a phone call that really could wait? Could you use social media differently? Could you present your ideas in ways that are most comfortable to you? Wear your own clothes?

Taking Action

In the following worksheet (see table 3), take a moment to self-assess your public leadership today. Alternatively, write your answers in a notebook or make a voice recording of them.

TABLE 3. Public leadership self-assessment worksheet

QUESTION	ANSWER	WHAT'S THE REASON?	CHOOSE ONE WORD FROM THE LIST TO DESCRIBE WHERE YOU ARE NOW: LEAD, LIVE, LOVE, WISH, WONDER, WAIT.
Example: When was the last time you conducted an on-camera interview?	2 years ago	I don't like doing TV interviews.	Wonder (where my limits are instead of pushing myself to do things that are uncomfortable)
If you add up your total number of followers on all social media platforms (Twitter, Facebook, LinkedIn, Instagram, other), how many do you have?			
What is the largest audience to which you've spoken in public?			
When was the last time you volunteered or were asked to speak or present in public?			

QUESTION	ANSWER	WHAT'S THE REASON?	CHOOSE ONE WORD FROM THE LIST TO DESCRIBE WHERE YOU ARE NOW: LEAD, LIVE, LOVE, WISH, WONDER, WAIT.
Do you feel well prepared and fully confident when you speak in public (meetings, webinars, organizational presentations)?			
What tools are you using to get your ideas out into the world?			
How often are you writing to get your ideas out there? Or using live video to share your point of view?			
How are you making sure that your work is recognized?			
What is the most prominent news outlet on which you have been invited to speak?			
What platforms are you creating for other women leaders to show up more fully?			

© Denise Padín Collazo

As you review your answers, what reactions do you have? Do you see any patterns?

_____

_____

_____

If you were to do three things in the next ninety days to grow your public profile, what might they be? (Here are some suggestions to generate ideas for you.)

➞ Ask for an opportunity to present at a staff meeting.

➞ Volunteer to write a four-hundred-word blog post on a subject you know well.

➞ Apply to create a small group at an upcoming conference.

➞ Explore a new social media platform.

➞ Take at least thirty minutes to prepare for the next speaking role you play and see what happens.

Now it's your turn! Write down your ideas in the spaces in figure 8 or in a notebook, or make a voice recording of your ideas.

1. _____

2. _____

3. _____

FIGURE 8. Three things I could do in the next ninety days to grow my public profile

Who will you tell about this goal, and how will you be held accountable to it?

What barriers can you anticipate that could prevent you from achieving these goals?

Hermana, what got you this far may not take you to the next step in your journey. Our communities, our country, and our world need you to stand up, hold your head high, and show up as your fullest, most loving, strong self. Through all the trials and struggles in our histories, our abuelas, tías, hermanas, and madres have made impossible choices to secure the future for generations to come. One day, someone will call you ancestor. What will they say about you when you're gone?

Showing Up in Public

Last year, I had the privilege of seeing Marc Anthony in concert. Being Boricua, I knew that people were going to dress *up* for this event. I bought a new dress, paired it up with a bad pair of heels, and marched all the way to my highly coveted row eleven seat like I owned the place. We Latinos *did* own the place that evening. It was a night of celebrating our cultures. I chuckled when I saw hipsters dressed too casually— wearing jeans, T-shirts, and casual shoes. They didn't know the Latino code. Seeing Marc Anthony wasn't just a concert, it was party time!

In the same way we prepare ourselves (hair, makeup, nails, brows, lashes, lipstick, clothes, shoes, hoop earrings) for a night of fun and dancing, we need to prepare in a slightly different way when our public-leader self shows up. Here are some things I've started to do to prepare for unfamiliar events. I request an attendee list and do a little research on the other people attending. I dress the part. I decide who the key people are that I'd like to connect with, and make it a priority. Because of my quick Google and LinkedIn searches, when I turn around and find myself standing face to face with a complete rock star, I can reference their latest book, the research they're leading, or the thing they're most interested in. It's easier to find good conversation starters with people since I've taken a minute to learn a little about them. It took Gabrielle Dolan, a global thought leader, telling me I *had* to create a LinkedIn profile and steadily grow my following for me to actually do it. I viewed that as self-promoting, and I was deeply resistant. But I have learned that if I want our people to win, I have to be willing to lead with everything I've got. Sometimes that means leading from the front (and investing in mundane tasks like building a social media page).

"You Don't Laugh at How You Fall; You Applaud How You Get Up"

Just like Marc Anthony, Jennifer Lopez is comfortable leading from the front. Ten years ago she fell on her butt in front of the whole world while she was performing at the American Music Awards.[11] The artist will.i.am was asked during an interview shortly after the show to comment on her fall.[12] After watching the replay a couple of times, he gave a wry smile and said, "She didn't fall, that's a move. It's called the pop-up!" He went on to explain to the reporters, "When I saw that, it was execution. She's devoted and she came out of it and still rocked it. So you have to applaud how you come up. You don't laugh at how you fall; you applaud how you get up. And she got up, boom!"

Sometimes, like JLo, we need to take the risk. And sometimes when we lead from the front, we fall down. Her performance didn't go exactly as she had planned, but it was still incredible. Instead of playing it safe, she chose a tricky move that involved high risk.

And here we are still talking about it today!

DISRUPTING ANTI-BLACKNESS IN YOUR CULTURE OF ORIGIN

The heartbeat of racism is denial,
the heartbeat of antiracism is confession.

IBRAM X. KENDI

We thrive in the fight by stewarding with others the movement for change and modeling authentic racial solidarity. Latinos of every racial identification need to fully acknowledge our own cultural history and call out anti-Blackness if we want to change the world.

Puerto Ricans and Our Blackness: It's Complicated

As a Latinx who is seeking to thrive in the fight for change, I've been doing a lot of reflecting on the role of anti-Blackness in my experience and in the Latinx community more broadly. In this chapter, I'll share stories about what I am learning in this process of exploration. I don't propose to have answers, mostly questions. I hope you will take time for your own inquiry as you read along.

Recently, I saw a mural in Yauco, Puerto Rico. The captivating girl and the artist's treatment of her demonstrate a perfect example of the relationship that Puerto Rico has with its own Blackness. The little girl seems to be drawn in an attempt to represent the racial mix that makes up the Puerto Rican identity (African, Native, and Spanish). Yet, the artist chose to give the girl one blue eye and one green eye. I asked myself, why not at least one brown eye, which is much more common and genetically likely. By choosing to draw one blue eye and one green eye, the artist, while attempting to represent the racial mix, skews toward whiteness.

In our family and in Puerto Rican culture in general, light features, light eyes receive greater attention and are viewed as more beautiful. One of my cousins has piercing blue eyes and is known by the family as "el nene lindo." What message does this send to the other family members whose hair and features are equally beautiful in their darkness?

This topic is addressed in Toni Morrison's classic *The Bluest Eye*, in which the main character, Pecola Breedlove, constantly receives the message of how her dark skin color and mannerisms relegate her to the status of "ugly." This societal perception causes her to wish she had blue eyes, essentially wishing she were white. This aspiration and society's treatment of her causes her eventually to go mad.

When I was in college, I came to my family hometown for Thanksgiving. After the meal, it's customary for us to gather around and tell stories. As we were in our circle, one of my half-white, half-Puerto Rican little cousins who presents as white walked past the circle of adults carrying a Black baby doll. Despite that we are racially mixed Puerto Ricans, the image of my cousin carrying around a Black baby doll sparked surprise, laughter, and lots of conversation. Jokes followed about where the doll came from, why the little "white" child was carrying around a Black baby doll.

By then, I had already begun to dig into multiracial organizing through the Harvard Foundation for Interracial and Intercultural Affairs with my mentor Dr. S. Allen Counter. I had started to develop a racial consciousness, and as the family discussion developed, I found myself feeling more and more uneasy.

One family member asked why Black people talk differently and say things like "cent" instead of "cents." Eventually, the conversation came around to dating and marriage. I started asking all my aunts if they would be good with their daughters or sons marrying someone who identified as Black. Mind you, many of us in our family would fit in just fine at many Black family gatherings due to our skin coloring, hair color, hair texture, features, and mannerisms. One by one, each of my aunts said that they would be opposed to their children marrying a Black man or woman. I was deeply distressed, so I called my Dad into the room. Surely, I thought, given his Bronx upbringing and his slightly darker skin tone, he'd have my back. I said, "Dad, would you be okay with me marrying a Black man?" I was shocked when he said no. Of course, he has given me permission to share this story and has come a long way since then in his journey.

The Roots of Anti-Blackness Run Deep

This was an early realization of the deep roots of anti-Blackness that live in my Puerto Rican family, like in many families who consider themselves Latino. Being Puerto Rican is by definition a racial mix. Three people groups came together in Puerto Rico via the conquest. The Arawak (Taino) native people, African slaves, and Spanish administrators together form most of the genetic pool of Puerto Ricans. Yet, despite this fact, 80 percent of Puerto Ricans on the 2010 census identified as white.[1] Like many

Puerto Ricans, my beloved family members were showing racial prejudice that seemed incongruent with their deeply held Christian beliefs. They were distancing themselves from Blackness and aligning themselves with whiteness. Isabel Wilkerson describes this dynamic in her book *Caste: The Origin of our Discontents*. In America's caste system, one of the rites of passage of immigrants and people who live between the poles of white and Black is to establish their position in society by distancing themselves from those in the lowest social caste. In America, she argues, the lowest caste is occupied by those deemed to be Black.[2]

My first response to this story is shame. Why was my racially mixed family distancing itself from the Blackness that we so proudly proclaim is part of the Puerto Rican experience? And why was this the first time I had noticed it? Natalia M. Perez describes this generational shame that causes many Latinx families to focus most of their energy on survival and assimilation instead of self-actualization and self-discovery in her article "On Generational Shame: Why Many Latinos Won't Admit They're Black, Too."[3] Her parents, like mine, were trying to figure out how to survive and navigate this new world. My parents made sure I spoke English very well from the beginning to avoid me having the difficult early experiences they had with not knowing the language at school. They named me Denise, which is not a typically Spanish-sounding name. Whether they did these things intentionally or unconsciously, the impact on me is still the same. I grew up in white churches, attending and excelling in schools that were informed by whiteness, and graduating from one of the country's most elite white institutions, Harvard University. Their focus was fitting in and getting ahead in the new white world in which they had arrived.

How can I claim to be a fighter for racial justice and have this kind of experience in my family? Over the years I have come to know and understand that I belong in the fight. I am not perfect, and I am worthy. Brené Brown, a researcher who has popularized the study of shame, says, "You either walk into your story and own your truth, or you live outside of your story, hustling for your worthiness."[4] This is me; this is who I come from and how I was raised. We've all been taught things that were wrong. I am committed to leading from my whole authentic self. This means accepting realities I can't change and changing those I can.

By naming and acknowledging the fact that I grew up in institutions that were informed by colonized thinking, colorism, and approximating whiteness (including my own family), I'm acknowledging the whole truth of who I am. This acknowledgment opens up space for my loved ones in the social justice world to see me more fully. It also creates space for people to explore their own personal experiences with anti-Blackness and the mark it has left on them.

Truths about Being Latino

There is very little that all Latino people have in common. It is important to understand that there are many different experiences of Latino communities that often get lumped together as one. It's actually inaccurate to talk about "the Latino community." It's more accurate to say "Latino communities" because there is such great diversity among people who are labeled as Latino or Hispanic.

Hispanic people don't all come from the same country; we don't eat the same food; we don't even all speak the same language. The only thing that binds all Hispanic people together is our shared experience of colonization, extraction, exploitation, family separation, and forced migration. *Most* people of Hispanic descent identify first as being from their country of origin: Mexican, Salvadoran, Cuban. People who are born here may add "American" to the end of their identifier (Puerto Rican American, Mexican American), or some people call themselves by names like Chicano or Boricua. If you're trying to figure out how to address our communities in general, the safest way for you to do this is to use either Hispanic or Latino, which are the general terms. If you're addressing a woman, you can say Latina or Hispanic woman. The word Latinx has also recently emerged as a gender-neutral way of acknowledging the intersectionality of being Latino, but it is not widely accepted.

> **The only thing that binds all Hispanic people together is our shared experience of colonization, extraction, exploitation, family separation, and forced migration.**

The United States is facing tectonic demographic shifts. In his classic book, *Open Veins of Latin America: Five Centuries of the Pillage of a Continent*, Eduardo Galeano lists the riches that have been extracted by the British Empire (and later the US) from Latin America, Central America, and the Caribbean. The list includes gold, silver, cacao, cotton, rubber, coffee, fruit, sugar, petroleum, iron, aluminum ore, and other minerals. But the most precious resource that has been extracted from all of us is *blood*.

Three Concurrent Realities about Being Latino

There are three separate realities that operate at the same time for us as Latinxs. First, according to political scientist Dr. Matt Barreto, most Latinos consider themselves a racial group. Latinos are actually an ethnic group, but that doesn't matter because many Latinxs, and the broader public, think Latinos are a racial group. Second, an overwhelming majority of Latinos believe that anti-Latino racism is growing in the United States. Third, the Latinx community has yet to fully notice, name, and disrupt the deep core of anti-Blackness that courses through every Latinx group. Until we as Latinas own all three of these realities at the same time, we are limiting our collective power. None of us are free until all of us are free.

Five hundred years ago, Christopher Columbus landed in the Americas and stole land from seventy million of our Indigenous loved ones, who were living on these continents in highly developed urban and rural centers. Waves of conquerors tried and failed to whitewash, kill, and erase our Native loved ones. To put that into perspective, today, approximately seventy million people live in the states of California and Texas combined. At the same time, millions of African people were forcibly stolen from their homes; brought to this continent; bred, bought, and sold as property; tortured, maimed, and killed in the name of religion and commerce. Black and Indigenous labor has been taken via slavery, and our bodies have migrated to the north to be used for cheap labor even to this day. That is the single link we all share, a history of oppression.

Imagining a More Authentic Future Together

Imagine if Black and Latinx families could come together in truly authentic ways. What if Black and Latinx families stood together at school board meetings in your community, or city hall? In Minnesota, Doran Schrantz, who leads Faith in Minnesota, has begun creating a multiracial governing coalition where Muslim, Black, white, and Latinx communities wrestle with each other to create policies that benefit everyone, instead of allowing communities to be pitted against each other. Even more, imagine if our communities in your city started voting as a bloc. In your state. In this country. Imagine what could change.

Despite all the talk about building multiracial power, very few people are actually doing this on the daily. It's hard work, and it happens in individual relationships, in small groups, and with intention. Black and Brown communities have been set up to compete for few resources. For example, in Flint, Michigan, after the North American Free Trade Act passed, big auto companies shipped jobs from Michigan to Mexico to take advantage of cheap labor. The Act also allowed companies to flood the Mexican market with excess corn. Farmers who had been subsisting finally abandoned their farms and migrated from Mexico to the US. When some ended up in Flint as Mexican immigrants, they and other Latinos were blamed for the loss of Black jobs in the auto industry. These divisive narratives persist until people come together, hear one another's stories, and realize that the real enemy doesn't even live in their neighborhood. When we are under the white gaze, we fall into the same old trap of being pitted against other folks of color. That script is old and tired.

Disrupting the Old, Tired Script

Despite the Latinx community's stated desire to build better relationships with our siblings in US Black communities, there are too few Latinas and even fewer Afro-Latinas leading in the movement. Even when we are present, many Latinas operate in less than full capacity in cross-racial spaces. At times, hermana, we haven't done the pre-work ourselves to have an honest talk about the role of anti-Blackness in the Latinx community (or in whatever our culture of origin may be). When we Latinxs or other communities fail to acknowledge it, we miss out on opportunities to build deep, loving, trusting relationships with leaders in the mosaic of individuals who make up the US Black communities.

A cadre of Black women are holding it down in the movement. They are showing up and leading from the front. They are inspiring other women to do the same. They are calling out anti-Blackness in the broader culture. They include Alicia Garza, cofounder of Black Lives Matter; Rosa Clemente, the first Black Puerto Rican to run for vice president of the United States; Ifeoma Ike, Esq., cofounding principal of Think Rubix; LaTosha Brown, who cofounded Black Voters Matter; Phyllis Hill, the national director of organizing for Faith in Action; Nse Ufot, executive director of the New Georgia Project; Ashley Shelton, executive director of Louisiana's Power Coalition; and others. In Detroit, Alia Harvey-Quinn organizes the people most of society casts out. She describes her organizing as being at the "mud roots" level because she says there's no grass where she organizes. She centers the leadership of young people trying to make a living in an economy that steers them toward crime. She organizes men and women who are returning from incarceration, Muslim women, as well as some who've left organized religion in disgust.

Evil Twins: White Privilege and Anti-Blackness

White privilege and anti-Blackness are evil twins. Anti-Blackness cannot exist without white privilege. White privilege cannot exist without anti-Blackness. Yet, when conversations about race and white supremacy are played on either/or terrain, Mestizos and lighter skinned Latinos (who look like me), and Latinas especially, tend to fade into the woodwork. Yet we can't afford to have anyone on the sidelines, because the biggest danger facing our country is the possibility of many, many light-skinned Latinos (who look and talk like me) assimilating and passing over into the white community. I've seen it happen in my family. I myself could easily pass and align myself with whiteness. Certainly, I've done so in the past, knowingly or unknowingly. It doesn't serve our movement or the possibility for radical change in this country for us to ignore this reality anymore.

If you are light skinned, you probably have some work to do to identify and combat your own anti-Blackness and name your privilege. I encourage you to use that privilege to clear ground for your Afro-Latinx sisters. If you identify as Afro-Boricua, Afro-Cubana, or Afro-Latina, you have the opportunity to remind us of the internalized racial oppression that causes so many of our people to long for whiteness. But it is not the job of Black Latinos to do the work for the whole Latino community. This is all of our responsibility. As we open our hearts, true, deep, loving, authentic cross-racial relationships of trust and love can grow. Only then can we build an authentic future together.

As women, we've led our families through unimaginable hardships. Let's apply these same gifts to thriving in the fight, stepping out, and leading to create that future world we've wished for but haven't yet seen. Because of our central leadership in our families, deepening the relationships of Black and Latino communities in the US can be transformed by women. In particular, I believe we as Latinas hold the keys to deep healing if we choose to use them.

La Chancleta Está en Nuestras Manos

In order to become whole, the Latinx community must come to terms with its own anti-Blackness and colorism. Who better to lead our communities into this than us Latinas? Hermana, la chancleta está en nuestras manos. Spanish is my second language, so I'll translate for all of my precious siblings who, like me, trip over our tongues when speaking Spanish. It means, the slipper is in our hands. Or maybe it would translate to "the ball's in our court," or "it's our move." I don't know about you, but my Abuela Lela used to threaten me with a cocked-slipper-in-hand when I misbehaved. She'd threaten a chancletazo, which is a swat with a flimsy slipper. I don't remember the chancleta ever actually connecting with my behind. Just the threat of it would straighten me up. I use the image of the chancleta because it's something we can all relate to. My point is that it's on us Latinas to do this work with ourselves. Change must not be solely dependent on the work of Afro-Latinx or Black loved ones.

> **The most important change we as Latinas could make is to notice, name, and disrupt the anti-Blackness that exists in our culture, our consciousness, our families, and ourselves.**

The most important change we as Latinas can make is to notice, name, and disrupt the anti-Blackness that exists in our culture, our consciousness, our families, and ourselves. We need to use all of our might to defeat that anti-Blackness. Unless we do this, we will not be whole people. Nor will we be capable of building deep relationships of sisterhood, daughterhood, or cousinhood with African American women who are anchoring the movement for social change today and, frankly, always have been. Together, Black and Latinx communities comprise over one hundred million people in the US, a country of approximately 320 million. Imagine how strong we would be if we stood together.

If you have a relationship with someone that by definition requires them to constantly ignore or excuse a gap in your worldview, that gets tiresome. So often, as members of the Latinx community, we celebrate our cultural Latin-ness, but there is zero acknowledgment of the role race and skin color plays in our various experiences of the world. By not naming this or calling it out, we're limiting the depth of the relationships we can have with other change agents. And we are limiting our own wholeness as people.

In the wake of the modern-day lynching of George Floyd, I coauthored with Stephanie Valencia an opinion editorial in the *Miami Herald*.[5] We wrote it on behalf of forty leaders of national Latino organizations. In it, we called for all Latinxs to do four things:

1. Clearly state that Black Lives Matter, and follow the lead of Black youth who are leading.

2. Call upon elected officials to not stand in the way of bold systemic transformation.

3. Invest in disrupting anti-Blackness in ourselves and our own organizations.

4. Call out Spanish language news sources like Univisión and Telemundo for their racially insensitive and culturally incompetent coverage of the rebellions of the spring and summer of 2020.

The letter was written by Latinas who are lighter skinned, and we ran it by our sisters and brothers who identify as Afro-Latinx, as well as Black partners. We did not put the work on them. Much of the change that needs to happen in Latinx communities cannot be dependent upon Black work.

In Puerto Rican literature, there is a classic poem called "Y tu agüela, aonde ejtá?" by Fortunato Vizcarrondo. Roughly translated, it means, "Where's your granny?" It challenges the racial hierarchy of Puerto Rico through a conversation between two Puerto Rican men, one with white-presenting features and the other who presents as Black. The Black Puerto Rican continually asks the light-skinned Puerto Rican why he shows off his wavy-haired children, yet never takes his grandmother out. In the final stanza the truth comes out: "you hide her in the kitchen because she's truly black."

In this poem, the white Puerto Rican was in denial. Ibram X. Kendi says "The heartbeat of racism is denial, the heartbeat of antiracism is confession."[6] When we confess and acknowledge the anti-Blackness in ourselves and in our world, we open up space for real conversations to happen, real relationships to emerge. There are many commonalities in our experiences, such as the many words we use to describe skin color. According to the Brazilian Institute of Geography and Statistics, Brazil has 136 terms to define skin color, but most of them are used to distance themselves from Blackness.[7] Here are a few of the 136 words they use:

Alva escura: Dark snowy white

Alvinha: Snowy white

Amarelosa: Yellowy

Azul: Blue

Bem clara: Very pale

Branca-morena: White but dark-skinned

Branca-palida: Pale white

Branquica: Whitish

Bronze: Bronze-colored

Bronzeada: Sun-tanned

Cardao: Colour of the cardoon, or thistle (blue-violet)

Cobre: Copper-colored

Cor-de-leite: Milk-colored (i.e. milk-white)

Cor-de-ouro: Gold-colored i.e. golden)

Cor-de-rosa: Pink

Esbranquecimento: Whitening

Escura: Dark

Fogoio: Having fiery-colored hair

Galega: Galician or Portuguese

Galegada: Somewhat like a Galician or Portuguese

Cafe: Coffee-colored

Cafe-com-leite: Cafe au lait

Marrom: Brown

Meio-amarela: Half-yellow

Meio-branca: Half-white

Meio-morena: Half dark-skinned

Meio-preta: Half-black

Melada: Honey-colored

Mulata: Mulatto girl

Loira-clara: Light blonde

Palida: Pale

Parda: Brown

Parda-clara: Light brown

Parda-preta: Black-brown

Pouco-clara: Not very light

Tostada: Toasted

Trigo: Wheat

Much like Brazilians and other Latinx cultures have many words to describe skin color, the American Black community can relate and name powerful, similar life experiences. Take, for example, the household brown paper bag. There was a time not long ago when admission to Black-owned night clubs and even Black churches was determined by whether a person's skin was lighter or darker than a brown paper bag.[8] People lighter than the brown paper bag were admitted; those with skin darker than a brown paper bag were denied admission.

Hope for the Future

This country is in a moment of both existential crisis and unmatched possibility. The undeniably violent attacks against Black Americans are on full view. The Latinx community is also under attack, and it's only a matter of time before more people will find themselves targeted. People need leadership. Many freeze, assume that someone else is leading change, and choose not to invest their vision, power, and leadership.

We need to invite as many people as possible into the fight for social change.

The Latinx population in this country has grown to fifty-nine million. The sixth most common last name in the US is García, according to the 2010 US Census as quoted by El Mundo.[9] At the same time as the Latinx population is growing, the communities that make up the Latino population in our country are developing an increasingly shared identity.

Dr. Matt Barreto, professor of political science and Chicana/o studies at University of California, Los Angeles, and founder of Latino Decisions, suggests Latinos are coming together in their concern for the attacks against our various people groups. Latino voters are connecting the dots between President Trump's proposal to build a border wall to "stop the infestation" of people coming across the border, the United States' failed response to hurricanes and earthquakes in Puerto Rico, and the president's references to "shithole" countries. Latinos are noticing a growing pattern of enmity.

After the El Paso shooting of 2019, Stephanie Valencia, who cofounded and leads a national polling and political strategy firm called EquisLabs, and a group of other nationally recognized Latinxs penned the following opinion piece in the *Washington Post*:[10]

> Many will not want to hear or believe this: Hispanics in this country are under attack. Black and brown people in this country are under attack. Immigrants in this country are under attack. And President Trump is fanning the flames of hate, division and bigotry directed at us all—immigrants and U.S. citizens alike. Though the attack has been pervasive for many people in this country for years, it is becoming an epidemic that is quickly infecting more communities and posing a real threat to our country. The president is also providing cover for white nationalists, explicitly endorsing hate speech and tacitly endorsing violence.

Lead into Your Vision

In times of great chaos where there is no known solution, the only answer is to innovate. I heard Ibram X. Kendi speak in December 2019. He's quoted at the beginning of this chapter and is the award-winning author of *Stamped from the Beginning: The Definitive History of Racist Ideas in America* and *How to Be an Antiracist*. He ended his remarks by reminding us that a few years before slavery ended in America, and a few years before Haiti was liberated from France, the people who were living in chattel slavery would never have imagined that it would soon end. He reminded us, "There's no other option than creating the impossible." Sometimes, when you think the finish line is so far away, it's just around the next corner. We need to keep leading into our proposed vision of the future.

Live into the Fullest Version of You

By acknowledging that you don't know everything about people from other racial or cultural groups, you create the opportunity to learn. It's hard to fill a cup that's already full. Surrendering in the fight is the opposite of living into the fullest version. Surrendering in the fight to disrupt anti-Blackness is to wonder what you don't know. For example, after many years of having heard my Black colleagues talk about Juneteenth, it wasn't until after the George Floyd murder that I took time to look it up for myself to understand why June 19th, 1865, was important as the official date when slavery ended in the United States. Two and a half years after slavery was declared illegal, it took a US general to be dispatched to Texas to let people know that slavery had ended. If you do nothing to educate yourself, you are surrendering in the fight. There are many resources you can explore to grow and learn.

Love Past Negatives That Hold You Back

When we each take responsibility for building stronger Black/ Latino partnerships, we will all become more whole, our movement will grow stronger, and it will have an impact on our country. When we take responsibility for doing our own internal, personal work to uncover the roots of anti-Blackness that live in our own consciousness, we loosen the negative grip that colonized thinking has on us. When we take responsibility for knowing our own story and learning the story of others, we build the possibilities for deeper, family-like relationships with others in our movement.

Take Action: The website *BlackLivesMatter.com* has a resources section with materials in English and Spanish.[11] The website *Ally.tools* has an "Antiracist Allyship Starter Pack" where you can begin.[12] You can download a simple tool from my website, *DeniseCollazo.com*, called "Noticing, Naming, and Disrupting Anti-Blackness in Your Culture of Origin."[13] There is a wealth of trainings, books you can read, respected organizations, movies you can watch to learn things that you don't know. It's on you to learn. It is not anyone's job to teach you.

Try On Something New

Recently, I was invited to address a national cohort of community organizers convened by Andrea Marta, national director of Faith in Action Fund, Phyllis Hill, national director of organizing for Faith in Action, and Dr. Joy Cushman, who helped develop the 2008 volunteer organizing model that Barack Obama used to fuel his first winning presidential campaign. The conveners were a high-powered team of women, to say the least. The subject of the conversation was "Building Independent Political Power in the Latinx Community."

Andrea, Phyllis, and Joy have intentionally created a safe, multiracial learning space among a group of the nation's most talented activists. In weighing out what to say, I followed the prompting of Andrea and the support of Phyllis to take a risk by naming the deep core of anti-Blackness that exists in the Latino community. This was a new move for me. I tried it on.

As I shared from my point of view as a white-presenting, US born, Puerto Rican woman, I offered questions, not answers. I told stories that I had in the past felt ashamed about. In preparing for the presentation, I had to be brutally honest with myself about the many ways that I had been taught to distance myself from Blackness by my culture, my family, my music, and even my church. I walked organizers through songs that reinforce racist tropes in popular Spanish language music. I told them about the many words that are used to describe skin color in our culture.

On a deeper level, I reflected on the pervasive ways that colonized thinking creates distance between us and our Indigenous and Black ancestors. I acknowledged the ways that in the past, I had reinforced a preference for whiteness. For example, I shared how while running a ballot measure in Florida in 2012, when we started calling voters who were the most regularly ignored, our leaders and staff were having little success hitting the numbers to which we had become accustomed. Because communities of color are ignored by most candidates and campaigns, their data is not kept up in the systems. Our outreach could have perhaps been the only outreach these voters were receiving. Instead of taking the time to really dig in and think about why our calling was taking longer as we reached out to our loved ones of color, we kept the focus on hitting numbers and winning in the heat of the campaign. I had made the call to keep driving toward numbers, instead of doing the harder work of including newer voters who no one else tries to reach. I made a choice to limit our outreach to the people with whom we could have had the most impact, in exchange for our numeric goals and winning the measure. This is one of my greatest regrets. We centered winning by calling more-likely-persuadable white voters and shortchanged the very people we propose to represent.

Yet, as I shared my experience with other organizers, I saw something incredible happen. A whole new level of conversation emerged with the organizers who were part of the conversation. Latinx organizers said things I had never heard them say before. They talked about the fact that all of the actors on Spanish language television and telenovelas are light skinned with blonde hair and light eyes. They described how their neighborhood grocery store still sells skin bleaching cream. My fellow Latinx leaders acknowledged the words that Spanish speakers use to describe members of the US Black community. Although it was a powerful and emotionally charged subject, people engaged in a deep and personal way.

I believe that conversations like this open up the kind of space where true relationships of trust can emerge. It requires that we are careful; even if we fall down, we'll get back up together and keep struggling on this journey toward freedom.

Will you take steps to prepare yourself to start making the impossible possible?

> *Behold, I am about to do something new;*
> *even now it is coming. Do you not see it?*
> *Indeed, I will make a way in the wilderness*
> *and streams in the desert.*
>
> ISAIAH 43:19

5

LEADING CLEAR ON PURPOSE

T here are many obstacles to building a new future. That is why being really clear about your purpose is so critical to your work. Often, your clarity of purpose is what keeps you thriving and not surrendering in the fight for change.

LEADER PROFILE

Heather Cabral

***Managing Director of Communications
at Faith in Action***

Heather Cabral is clear about her purpose. She has dedicated her life to elevating the stories of everyday people in the media as part of the fight for racial justice in her role as senior director of communications at West End Strategy. This passion and clarity about her purpose provides the energy that fuels her, news cycle after news cycle, to fight for real change for people who are constantly fighting just to live.

(continues)

(continued)

Heather comes from royal activist lineage. You see, she is a cousin of Amílcar Cabral, who the *Washington Post* describes in this way:[1]

Amílcar Lopes Cabral was a Pan-Africanist revolutionary and thinker who "masterminded the end of Portuguese rule in Guinea-Bissau and Cabo Verde," two West African countries that were Portuguese colonies until their independence was recognized in 1974 and 1975, respectively. Cabral was born in Guinea-Bissau of parents from Cabo Verde, went to university in Portugal and was assassinated in Conakry, Guinea, from where he was leading the revolution for independence.

On June 9, 2020, Heather's fight became even more personal when her young cousin was assaulted by an adult in his neighborhood in Florida. The next day, she told me, "We just celebrated his high school graduation. He's a quiet gentle kid in a huge body. He played basketball for his high school and is going on to play in college as well. He's such a good kid. People don't know that he still calls his mom 'Mommy.' For his graduation, I bought him a portable Ninja blender for his dorm. He's all about clean eating. I asked his Mom if I should buy him protein shake mix and he told her, 'Mommy, you can't put that stuff in your body.'"

Heather has followed in the footsteps of her ancestors, who fought for freedom for Africans fifty years ago. She continues to this day telling stories in order to shift the narrative in the fight for social, economic, racial, and political change.

Leading Clear on Purpose

Shortly before she passed away in March 2020, I interviewed Beatriz Solis for this book. She had served as a director of Healthy Communities at the California Endowment. I asked her what compelled her to stay in the fight for change. She said, "I have an internal compass that is deep. I focus on the most impacted people. At my core, it steers me and how I use my personal time and focus to stay the course." I was struck by how important being really clear about her purpose was to Bea's impact on the world. Her purpose was her "north star." She came from humble means, and her family had to fight for everything they got. It is the foundation upon which she conducted her life's work.

She described that to go through the grueling, eight-year journey of getting a PhD at UCLA, "you have to have the gut feeling of why!" She described this achievement as a marathon, run in partnership with her husband Mohammad, who she described as her "rock," and her two sons that were born at UCLA. Bea understood that a win is just one step in a lifelong journey.

Making Change across the Country

When you are clear about your purpose, that clarity provides the fuel you need to continue thriving in the fight when the road becomes treacherous. Like Heather and Bea, there are thousands of other women and men of color who are leading with deep clarity about their purpose and winning real change for children and their families. Here are some examples.

In Alabama, a broad group of leaders including DeJuana Thompson from Think Rubix, LaTosha Brown from Black Voters Matter, Stephanie Strong from Faith in Alabama, and many others led the charge in 2018 to turn out Black voters in the US Senate election. There hadn't been a Democratic senator in Alabama in that senate seat in twenty-two years.

In Arizona, Alejandra Gomez and Tomás Robles Jr. from LUCHA led a group of mostly Latino young adults who had built a base by ousting Sheriff Joe Arpaio and then aimed that base at changing the political calculus in the state of Arizona.

In Virginia, Tram Nguyen was organizing with New Virginia Majority before organizing in Virginia was cool. Her Facebook feed lists legislative victories on the regular. She is winning in the fight and making material changes that benefit children and their parents.

> **When you are clear about your purpose, that clarity provides the fuel you need to continue thriving in the fight when the road becomes treacherous.**

Heather, Bea, DeJuana, LaTosha, Stephanie, Alejandra, Tomás, and Tram are leading clear on purpose. Communities are changing as a result of their leadership. In each case, grassroots leaders, organizers, and clergy tapped deeply into their sets of relationships and moved them with very little investment from the rest of the world. I often hear donors describe places that are in out-of-the-way areas (such as most of the rural South) by saying, "There's no infrastructure there." When people say that, here is what I hear: "There is no white-led infrastructure there." The truth is that our communities have known how to self-organize due to our lived experiences as enslaved and colonized people. Yet, typical observers of social change are still figuring out how to support these emergent efforts. Donors and other supporters are slowly shedding outdated mindsets about what to do when people in communities lead crystal clear on their purpose.

Even when we're told something is impossible, as activists, we don't give up. As a new organizer I was taught that "No" just means "Not now" or "That's not a priority." It's our job to make things priorities that weren't before. We walk a new path with others, and we sometimes feel surprised when we look around and see a team of powerful people around us who share the same vision.

When you are acting in alignment with your "true north" as Bea Solis would say, you are more likely to be thriving in the fight for change. When you have trouble finding your joy, that might be a sign that you're not leading clearly into your purpose, and that perhaps you may not be thriving, but instead surrendering.

When you are thriving, you do your best work despite setbacks you may face. When you are thriving in the fight, you are more able to speak your truth, and you are able to follow the lead of Black women who have been liberating our country since before its inception.

Speak Your Truth

Despite our leadership in family settings, many Latinxs have been trained by culture, family, faith, tradition, and even experience to serve humbly from behind the scenes and expect no recognition or acknowledgment. It takes courage and practice to speak our truth. It takes the discipline of taking a breath and reflecting on how you are feeling, not how you are thinking. It often requires an accountability partner who keeps you focused on your purpose.

It is imperative that women of color practice clearly expressing our point of view, while standing firmly grounded in our purpose and vision. When you find yourself feeling angry, for example, seek to identify the source of the anger. Because anger is a clarifying emotion. It helps you know when something is wrong. Anger can also point you to the pathway forward. Instead of getting down on yourself about feeling angry, think about what that anger is telling you about what is wrong and what needs to change.

Follow Black Women

Black women have been agents of liberation and freedom since before this country was founded. There are many examples to point to, including people like Ella Baker, Fannie Lou Hamer, Harriet Tubman, Rosa Parks, and scores of other women who have paved the way for current and future generations of leaders. In the literary world, Octavia Butler's Earthseed trilogy foreshadowed much of what we are seeing today. Written in 1998, the book *Parable of the Talents* describes the United States after its collapse.[2]

> People are addicted not only to designer drugs but also to "dream masks," which generate virtual fantasies as guided dreams, allowing wearers to submerge themselves in simpler, happier lives. News comes in the form of disks or "news bullets," which "purport to tell us all we need to know in flashy pictures and quick, witty, verbal one-two punches. Twenty-five or thirty words are supposed to be enough in a news bullet to explain either a war or an unusual set of Christmas lights." The Donner Administration has written off science, but a more immediate threat lurks: a violent movement is being whipped up by a new Presidential candidate, Andrew Steele Jarret, a Texas senator and religious zealot who is running on a platform to "make American great again."

This description of America sounds eerily accurate yet was written twenty-two years ago. In writing the Earthseed trilogy, Octavia Butler was clear about her purpose. Her purpose was to envision a future in which Black people didn't just exist but were central figures.

Many Black and Brown women have taught me how to challenge systems and how to do so while treating each other with deep love and concern. Had it not been for Black Americans, the United States may not have become a democracy. Nikole Hannah-Jones explains in her essay in the recent *New York Times Magazine* series entitled 1619, "Our democracy's founding ideals were false when they were written. Black Americans have fought to make them true."[3] Black people have driven every change to make this country more equal. This work has paved the way for the struggles of many other oppressed people groups, including many Latinos.

Yet so often, the voices of Black women and all women of color are muted and far from being centered. This needs to change if we have any chance of winning true liberation and equality in this country and beyond.

When you are clear on your purpose and you thrive in the fight for change, you can change more than policies, you can transform yourself, those around you, and the institutions to which you belong.

You Can Transform Your Organization

Our current institutions are not benefitting from the true brilliance of Black women, Latinxs, Indigenous women, Asian and Pacific Islander women, and all women of color. Often, women of color are paraded around for the appearance of diversity, but they don't hold true power and authority over critical decisions.

An article by David A. Thomas and Robin J. Ely, "Making Differences Matter," contends that organizations that are most able to leverage the full brilliance of a diverse team do the following three things:[4]

1. They encourage open discussion about cultural backgrounds.

2. They eliminate all forms of dominance (by hierarchy, function, race, gender, etc.) that inhibit full contribution.

3. They secure organizational trust.

Organizations must aspire to be transformed by the diverse points of view that come with having widely diverse leadership. Organizations must move beyond expanding diversity and simply trying to increase market share by hiring more people of color. Companies and institutions need to be willing to be transformed into something new by leaders of color. Often, this means that the white folk in charge need to step down, give up some of their privilege, and make room for fresh perspectives.

You Can Shape Better Decisions

Finally, when Latina change agents are recommending strategies, listen to them. Don't assume that because you've been around longer, you know what's best. Many times women of color in organizations tamp down our own instincts and defer to the "wisdom" of others in leadership. Yet, by suppressing the cultural wisdom and knowledge that women bring, we end up with solutions that are less effective. Women have their finger on the pulse of communities. Listen to them. A McKinsey study showed that "companies in the top-quartile for gender diversity on their executive teams were 21% more likely to have above-average profitability than companies in the fourth quartile."[5]

Leading clear on purpose is key to our successful leadership as women of color because that acknowledgment of a moral center gives us the strength and energy to persevere through all types of trials.

Leading clear on purpose requires that we *lead into our vision*. Oftentimes, by leading clear on purpose, we end up charting out new and unknown territory. The fact that you're putting forth a new point of view or proposing a new way forward can feel risky. And, there is also often no way to know whether the direction you're heading is the right direction until you've committed yourself. It's hard to point to data about why an approach will work when you have only your experience and intuition telling you to move in a new direction. Still, it is important to lead into your vision.

I spend much of my time partnering with people whose motivation is rooted in their faith and personal values. Faith is often defined in the Christian context as "the substance of things hoped for, the evidence of things not seen." As a person of faith, I usually think of faith as being the opposite of fear. Fear, like surrender, causes you to wish for a different future but never commit to it with your actions.

My godson Jair Marta is a disciplined young baseball player. In baseball, you need to commit to swinging before you know whether you'll actually hit the ball, but by building strength, power, and endurance through practice, you increase your odds of success over time.

Isabel Allende, niece of Chilean president Salvador Allende, is the author of *The House of the Spirits* and many other novels. She is one of the first Latin American woman novelists to gain critical acclaim. *The House of the Spirits* is one of the most famous books in the Latin American "magical realism" genre. I'm sure when she was starting out, she didn't know that her work would speak to so many people across the globe. She still kept writing.

Octavia Butler, the first Black woman to write in the science fiction genre, had to imagine worlds and events that had not yet existed. It's eerie to read the Earthseed trilogy today and observe how prescient our groundbreaking sister had been.

Taking Action

I encourage you to take time to reflect on how closely your everyday work and activities line up with your purpose, using the following worksheet (see figure 9).

Take a moment to fill out this worksheet. You can decide to fill it out for work, home, or personal spaces like friend groups or volunteer experiences. Check the boxes that apply to you.

I am taking a moment to assess how clear on purpose I am in my leadership.

I am taking a moment to assess how clearly I communicate my purpose in the following setting (fill in which area you're answering for; e.g., home, work, family, congregation, sports team, or other)_____ :

☐   When I put forth recommendations or requests, I usually ground them in my purpose and vision.

☐   When I make recommendations or requests, they are considered and often adopted by those around me.

☐   My actions reflect my purpose and vision.

☐   When I feel that a project or relationship is moving off track, I respond by seeking change, by rooting it in my purpose and vision.

☐   When I make suggestions or put forth recommendations, my ideas are attributed to me.

☐   When I put forth a strategy approach, it is considered with seriousness by others.

☐   When I trust my instincts and suggest an alternative approach (e.g., noting that a project or deadline may be unrealistic), my point of view is treasured and heeded.

☐   _____

☐   _____

Overall, when I lead clear on purpose, I have a positive impact on the lives of others.

| **1** | **5** | **10** |
| Never | Sometimes | All the time |

What can you learn from Heather Cabral, Isabel Allende, Jair Marta, and Octavia Butler about leading "clear on purpose"?

_____

FIGURE 9. Clear on purpose worksheet

Each of the leaders featured in this chapter have had immeasurable impact on their spheres of influence. They were incredibly gifted, and they leaned into honing their gift. They have made an impact on the entire world as their clarity of purpose, discipline, and giftedness merged together to create art. You can do this too. Dig into your gifts, live fully into your purpose, and watch the world change around you!

LEADER PROFILE

Tere Flores Onofre

Director of Organizing Sacramento Area
Congregations Together (ACT)
by Tere Flores

For over fifteen years, I have committed myself to fighting for social justice with communities that are exploited yet unseen. I started my career in Faith in Action (formerly PICO National Network) at the age of sixteen when I was hired as a youth organizer by the local affiliate in Contra Costa County. Even before I was a paid organizer, the Catholic youth group that I helped lead and grow was successfully organizing in and outside of our congregation. All of us were either immigrants or children of immigrants and our families had first-hand experience with systemic injustices: whether it was being undocumented, foregoing doctor's visits because of a lack of health insurance, or having wages stolen by unscrupulous employers. Organizing was personal for me and I embraced it not only as a job, but as my vocation and God's answer to my many questions.

(continues)

(continued)

Soon after I was hired, a new executive director came on board. He was bold, visionary, charismatic, spontaneous, and white. His hiring by our board of directors and with the support of our national network sent the message to me that he was a model for executive leadership. As my supervisor for most of my time with that organization, he was supportive and invested in my development. Yet, I struggled with seeing myself as a powerful leader and organizer because I did not look like him. I was a young (and short) brown woman with strong indigenous features. I had graduated at the top of my class, but because of my quiet and analytical character, I was rarely the first person to speak or share ideas. I saw so many differences between my boss and me that I almost gave up owning my God-given power.

Through deep discernment and thanks to fellow chingonas consistently pouring into me, I realized that I was already powerful and didn't need to emulate a white model of leadership. My mentoras helped me understand that my power comes from fully owning all my parts and leading with my whole authentic self. This meant loving both my roots (where I come from) and my branches (who I am becoming).

In my mid-twenties, it also meant embracing my identity as bisexual, first coming out to myself and eventually my friends, clergy leaders, colleagues, and family. This was transformative and I began to lead confidently in my personal and professional life in ways I didn't think were possible by redefining what a powerful leader looks like for myself and others. This journey hasn't been easy, but I'm clear on why I'm here and the leader I have been called to be.

(continues)

(continued)

These excerpts from the poem "Chingona Fire" by Angela Aguirre are my gift to all you *womyn* out there who need to hear some Chingona Fire right now.

Chingona

A chingona is any woman who chooses to live life on her own terms. PERIOD...

What truly defines us as chingonas is our ability to harness our fire...

Our Chingona fire to be exact. Chingona fire is a revolutionary act...

Chingona fire is the ability to convey an entire message with your eyebrows alone...

It is switching from Spanish to English mid conversation, zero fucks given...

It is loving yourself and taking no shit and refusing to apologize for your existence...

This poem is intended to speak to the chingona in you...

You. are. not. alone. I see you, mija. And you are fly as fuck. [6]

6

THRIVING BY RAISING MONEY

Most people hate asking other people for money. Yet, raising money is crucial to thriving in the work of social change. In the nonprofit world, raising money is supremely important. The people who raise the money usually call the shots. If you want to lead into your vision, you need money to do it.

I've included this chapter because in order to thrive in the fight for social, racial, political, and economic change, you must be able to raise money. This chapter will help you see how important fundraising is to your work and help you take steps to actively raise money, and it offers advice to prospective donors who may want to support your work.

I've had many opportunities to speak with the people who donate to our nonprofit organization. It is a wonderful experience! Recently, I was making calls to donors to thank them for their contributions. I got the opportunity to speak with one donor and hear his concerns and hear how his hopes and dreams line up with our work. The donor said back to me, "Thank *you*! I'm so glad to hear about all the great work that you guys are doing. Keep it up!" What a great shot of encouragement for me as a leader. I've learned that the best time to ask for money is when you've just raised money. As a result, at the end of the conversation, I asked him to consider giving more money, which he didn't mind at all.

It's easy for most people to avoid fundraising work. But once you get into it, it can be really fun and rewarding. That's what it feels like to thrive while raising money.

By inviting others to support the work, you are creating a pathway to a world into which they may have no other access. When you invite them to participate and give in more and in different ways, you are also creating pathways for them to thrive. Your donors can become your biggest promoters and champions, if you let them.

When you are thriving while raising money, you have a good feeling building relationships with your financial supporters. You have built strong, long-term relationships of trust with the people who give money to fuel your vision. They count on you to tell them the truth about what you are learning and what you need. You show up confidently to describe your work to people who have the ability to move resources. You feel joyful when you have the chance to share with philanthropists, corporate sponsors, individual members, and donors. When you're thriving while raising money, not only are you reaching out to donors, but they are reaching out to you, inviting you to apply for resources. Money is flowing to you and your work. You are helping others raise funds as well. And, you are also finding ways to generate repeatable income that supports your vision over the long haul.

Surrendering by Not Raising Money

Despite its critical importance, most people avoid and procrastinate on the tasks involved in raising money. This is what it looks like to surrender by not raising money. You wish you had more resources. You wonder where funds will come from, yet you dread picking up the phone to make fundraising phone calls. You wait to send that email. You wring your hands about the finances instead of putting asks out there.

One of the biggest nightmares in the nonprofit world is struggling to make payroll. Joshua Humbert, my colleague who is a national development professional and CEO of the Humbert Group, LLC, says "I love helping good organizations. And I hate seeing good organizations die." Perhaps the only nightmare worse than not making payroll is losing talented people because you don't have the money to pay them. As Latinas in the movement, you have to be able to generate revenue. It is a must. I encourage you to take steps to learn how to raise funds if you're not already doing so. If you are, I encourage you to take every opportunity to grow your skill in this area.

What It Takes to Thrive in Nonprofit Fundraising

In order to be successful and thrive in nonprofit fundraising, you need to have a strong *product*, you need tremendous *persistence*, and you need strong *positioning*.

Product

Let's start with the product. You need to have a strong *product* that you are promoting. The work you do and the impact you are having is your product. You can be the best fundraiser in the world, but if your work is not strong, you will have trouble raising funds to support it. People generally invest in things that they view as successful.

If you find yourself in a situation where you are having difficulty raising money and you know in your heart that the work you are doing is not as strong as it could be, it's best to acknowledge this and ask for help from trusted colleagues, past donors, potential donors, and others. Don't carry this burden alone. Fundraising is about people investing in people. Go to the people who love you and support what you're doing and ask them for their wisdom, help, and support.

Because you may be used to doing your work on a shoestring, it's easy to underestimate how much it'll cost to actually have the necessary staff, tools, and resources. Sometimes, you can't even imagine what having more resources might feel like. For example, if you could hire additional people to handle some of the things you do, could you be freed up to provide greater strategic guidance to the work? I've watched white organizers and Latina organizers hold similar leadership roles, yet I have noticed that often the white organizers assert their financial needs much more openly than Latinas and other women of color. You never know how much help is available to you unless you chart out what you really need and ask for it.

Persistence

In addition to having a strong product, you need to be doggedly *persistent* to succeed at fundraising. This may sound redundant, but in order to raise money, you need to ask for it—often! There is a direct correlation between time spent raising money and amount raised. I usually recommend to new executive directors to allocate at least one day per week every week to fundraising. When you are able to keep this kind of discipline, the reward usually comes in over time. If you are not a director but want to grow your fundraising skill, dedicate a certain amount of time to it each week.

> **Good fundraising involves impeccable follow up.**

When a donor shows interest in your work and asks for follow-up, it's supremely important to follow up as soon as humanly possible. I often try to respond that same day or within a very short period of time. Good fundraising involves impeccable follow up. When you have the attention of a donor, keep it. I say, "Strike while the iron's hot." Don't let follow-up tasks to donors sit on your to-do pile for weeks on end. This slows down momentum and delays fundraising decisions.

Persistence also means being willing to face a lot of rejection. If you are timid, have thin skin, or have issues with rejection, maybe fundraising is not the best role for you. When you raise money, you get used to hearing a lot of no's, a lot of non-responses, but when you get that yes, it makes it worth all the rejection.

As an example, Andrew Gillum ran for governor of Florida in 2018. He told me there were days when he'd spend eight hours making donor phone calls and not raise a single dollar. That's persistence. Despite the many days of striking out, in the end he raised $55 million for his historic race to serve as the first Black governor of Florida.[1] He believed in himself and his strength as a candidate, and he tapped into the many others who believe in him to mount a very successful race. In essence, he had the persistence to stay at it even when it was discouraging.

When you are raising money, it is rare that donors come to you. You need to go to them. If you are raising funds from a foundation or corporate source and you reach out and get no response, don't take it personally. They are rarely able to be as responsive as they might like. So, just reach out again, and again.

Positioning

Along with having a great product and being persistent, thriving by raising funds means investing energy in *positioning* you and your work in places where others will become aware of them. Because fundraising is about people giving money to people, you need to see yourself like a product and make sure you are positioned in the proper places. Think about the people who sell paletas or elotes in our communities. They have the product (the ice cream or corn on the cob), they persist (pushing the stand around or standing behind it for hours), and then they strategically position themselves (usually right outside the schoolyard after school). People can't buy your product if you're not strategically positioned.

Often, in the movement for social change, Latina change agents don't have fundraising or budget responsibility or authority. For reasons of our family histories with money and poverty, many women of color are uncomfortable with raising money. But they are often leading organizational efforts that require tremendous resources.

Other times, in the field of community organizing, Latinx activists avoid the fundraising roles and prefer to do "work on the ground." This is a false binary. You could be building people power, money power, and people's money power at the same time. Since you don't, you often end up carrying out strategies that other people (who are less familiar with your communities) cook up. You don't have real power to create, shape, or drive. You also don't advance into more executive roles because those positions usually require the ability to raise money.

Another important part of positioning is making sure that you are in the right places, building relationships with people who are making decisions about money. In philanthropy, this might mean being at the right conference, or knowing the right people. In corporate giving, it's about making sure you really understand the self-interests of the company. Sometimes you will have to admit to others that you need help with positioning and invite their help.

Especially as a woman of color, at times you will have to volunteer yourself to do things. If you wait until an invitation is explicitly made, you could be waiting a very long time. For example, you may need to work to get yourself to the right reception, or have others advocate for you to be invited to speak at a conference. You can invest in growing your social media following or ask for an introduction to a key prospective donor from someone you already know. If you don't spend time thinking about how to position yourself and your organization, others will position you where they think you belong.

A Word for Nonprofit Executive Directors

When you are the organizational leader, raising money is a sacred responsibility. People's lives and families depend on your ability to raise funds, communicate your financial position clearly to all, and be honest with staff and leaders about the finances. I'm grateful to my mentor Jim Keddy, who currently leads Youth Forward in Sacramento. He encouraged me in my first year of organizing to integrate fundraising as part of my organizing work. But I'd like to give a special shout-out to my very first mentor—my dad, Rafael Padín.

He grew up in the South Bronx, and he always had a hustle. He pitched pennies and ran numbers for the neighborhood bookie. When I was little, when we had candy sales or walk-a-thon fundraisers for school, he'd encourage me to go out into the neighborhood and knock on people's doors to ask for support. He taught me early on, "Denise, you'd better sell yourself, because if you don't, no one will do it for you!" Great life lesson.

There are times when women of color are not the executive leader, yet when they express to senior leadership the need for more resources to carry out the work, many nonprofit executives take the "Father knows best" approach and commit to raising funds or moving budget items around. By not engaging the change agents themselves in raising money, the activists' power is limited in the following ways. The change agents end up doing too much work with too little money; the organization is limiting the experience of emerging women of color because one of the key competencies for serving in higher leadership in organizations is fundraising skill. And, these executives are making an assumption that the communities themselves are too poor to be tapped to support the work that is being done.

This is a paternalistic approach that limits the success of our organizations and our organizers. When women are crying out for more resources, it's because they need them. Listen to them and engage them in the solution.

TIPS FOR DONORS WHO WANT TO INVEST IN LATINA LEADERSHIP

My colleague Aaron Dorfman is the president and CEO of the National Committee for Responsive Philanthropy. In an early conversation about this book, he encouraged me to include a list of tips for donors who want to support the work of Latina leaders. Here they are:

Tip 1: Don't wait for us to call you. We're usually overworked and very busy. Reach out to us by phone or text and be willing to talk to us while we're on the move.

Tip 2: Invite us many times. If you reach out to us and you don't hear back, it's because we're usually overworked and very busy. If you invite us to present at a conference and we say no, persist. I know many Latinas who have declined invitations to speak or be honored for their work because of the lessons we've been taught about humility and leading from behind without expecting any recognition or reward.

Tip 3: When we do call you, we've needed your help for a long time. Listen intently to what we need, and do your best to help us out.

(continues)

(continued)

Tip 4: Make it easy for us to access funds. Remember, many of us have complicated relationships with money. Instead of asking a close family member for a loan to support my exorbitant college tuition, my parents chose to move out of their house, work overtime, deliver Domino's pizza, and eventually declare bankruptcy.

Tip 5: Give us other ways to communicate with you. If you find that we are delaying at the point of the process where we need to submit something to you in writing, it's likely we worry that our writing isn't good enough. So instead of sending it over, many of us will wring our hands and avoid. To combat this, work to receive information in many modalities: PowerPoints, YouTube videos, listening into a meeting via phone, events, phone conversations, newspaper articles, etc.

Tip 6: Ask us how we are investing in our own development and consider paying for it in some way. Always take a moment to ask Latinas and women of color more broadly how they're investing in their own development. So often, women stay so busy doing the work that we put our own needs last. Ask what they'd love to learn but haven't had time for. Seek additional ways to support the leadership of women. A prestigious Kellogg fellowship includes funds for self-care for things like acupuncture and massage. Recently, the Ford Foundation started investing in gatherings that can be built around radical self-care. These are the kinds of supports that can rejuvenate Latinas and all women of color. Ask about the organization's leave and parental benefits policies, ask how they're preparing for retirement, etc. There are many ways to support the development of Latinas. Sometimes we're too busy to imagine what could be.

Thrive Not Surrender

Now, let's take time to apply the thriving (lead, live, love) and surrendering (wish, wonder, wait) concepts as they apply to money. Use the following chart (see table 4) to respond, or create your own on another piece of paper. Alternatively, make a voice recording of your responses.

TABLE 4. Moving from surrendering to thriving when raising money worksheet

RESOURCE	WHAT DOES THRIVING LOOK LIKE?	WHAT DOES SURRENDERING LOOK LIKE?
	What behaviors would you exhibit if you were to Lead into your vision, Live into your fullest self, and Love past negatives?	*What behaviors would you exhibit if you were to* Wish for a future reality, Wonder where your limits are, and Wait for solutions and permission to come from others?
Money (your personal money)	Lead into vision	Wish for a different future
	Live into fullest self	Wonder where your limits are
	Love past negatives	Wait for permission and answers to come from others

RESOURCE	WHAT DOES THRIVING LOOK LIKE?	WHAT DOES SURRENDERING LOOK LIKE?
Money (the money you need to get your job done)	Lead into vision Live into fullest self Love past negatives	Wish for a different future Wonder where your limits are Wait for permission and answers to come from others
Money (the money your organization needs)	Lead into vision Live into fullest self Love past negatives	Wish for a different future Wonder where your limits are Wait for permission and answers to come from others
Money (the money needed for your entire field)	Lead into vision Live into fullest self Love past negatives	Wish for a different future Wonder where your limits are Wait for permission and answers to come from others

© Denise Padín Collazo

Now that you've spent some time thinking about how the thriving not surrendering approach helps you consider ways to activate your leadership more fully, here's another exercise to try.

Taking Action

On a sheet of paper, draw three columns, one for a list of resources you have at your disposal, and one for the resources you need that you don't yet have. In the third column, write down the names of people who can help you get the resources you need. Or you can use the following chart (see table 5). Alternatively, make a voice recording of your responses.

TABLE 5. Moving from the money I have to the money I need worksheet

MONEY I HAVE	MONEY I NEED	NAMES OF PEOPLE WHO CAN HELP ME GET THERE
Example: $1,000 financial gift from Ximena Sanchez	10 more people to support us at that level	Ximena, Frank, Jasmine

MONEY I HAVE	MONEY I NEED	NAMES OF PEOPLE WHO CAN HELP ME GET THERE

© Denise Padín Collazo

As you lead into your vision and shape the work you want to do, people start to see you. They see a through line between you and your work; you start to grow your public profile. When that happens, fundraising gets easier. But it is never easy. Once you start to apply thriving energy to raising the money you need to carry out your vision, you will grow your impact and increase your ability to make change with and for the families in your community.

LEADER PROFILE

Andrea Marta

Executive Director
Faith in Action Fund
by Andrea Marta

I've heard stories about how my Great Grandmother Jovita Quiroz Rojo walked the 1,745-mile journey from Pueblo Nuevo, Durango, Mexico, to Decoto, California, in the San Francisco Bay Area. They worked in fields and restaurants along the way. She did all kinds of farm work, picking flat beans, harvesting plums, and picking tomatoes. I've learned how she raised her thirteen children as an immigrant woman. By far, my favorite story of her happened one day when she was working on the apricot pitting floor.

The women pitting the apricots got paid by the boxes of pits they filled. At times, my Great Grandma Jovita would bring my Grandma Gloria and her other siblings with her to help earn more money. Pitting is hard work, you use a curved knife that looks like a carpet cutter. It's important to cut around the outside of the pit exactly at the crease to remove the pit and not damage the apricot. They stood at a metal table doing this for hours on end. My grandma never mentioned taking breaks.

At the apricot pitting site, there was a particular worker who would come by and talk to my Grandma Jovita and others while they worked. Often, the woman would sneak off, having stolen a full box of pits from one of her coworkers. Everyone was paid by the box of pits they each turned in. She would do this as many times as it took for her to collect the number of boxes

(continues)

(continued)

she needed to get paid for the day. My Grandma Jovita caught her several times and told her to knock it off, and stop stealing. One day she had had enough. When the woman walked away with one of my great grandmother's full boxes of pits she told her to stop. The woman told them that the box was hers and to back off.

This woman was not only stealing the work my Grandma Jovita had put in but also the labor of her daughter (my Grandma Gloria), who had been helping her that day. My Grandma Jovita had to fight the woman for her box, and when it was all over every woman on the packing floor applauded my Great Grandma Jovita. They had all been tired of having their hard work stolen out from under them.

The fight I have deep inside of me isn't an accident, it's because the women before me have fought for their families and communities from day one. My fight comes from my ancestors, my Great Grandma Jovita, who stood up to a bully not only for herself but for her children and the women pitting apricots by her side.

Hearing this story about Great Grandma Jovita helped me see that many times we as women of color have our work stolen right out from under us. That's why it's important for me to raise the resources I need to support my vision for the work.

CONCLUSION

DRIVING TO A NEW FUTURE

Don't ask what the world needs.
Ask yourself what makes you come alive and go do that,
Because what the world needs is people
who have come alive.

HOWARD THURMAN

Un Caldero de Arroz

Every woman in my family has a special secret to cooking rice.

Remember in the movie *Forrest Gump* (I know, I'm old), when Forrest's friend Bubba recounted the many ways Bubba's family cooked shrimp?

> You can barbecue it, boil it, broil it, bake it, sauté it.
> There's uh, shrimp-kabobs, shrimp creole, shrimp
> gumbo. Pan fried, deep fried, stir-fried. There's pine-
> apple shrimp, lemon shrimp, coconut shrimp, pepper
> shrimp, shrimp soup, shrimp stew, shrimp salad, shrimp
> and potatoes, shrimp burger, shrimp sandwich . . .[1]

Rice is to us Puerto Ricans as shrimp was to Bubba and his family: arroz con gandules, arroz con camarones, arroz con jueyes, arroz con pollo, arroz con habichuelas, arroz con salchicha, arroz blanco, asopao, paella, and the Christmas classic arroz con dulce . . . and that's just the beginning.

Master cocineras like my Abuela Lela cooked yummy rice every time. She made it look easy!

Trust me, it isn't!

Our rice, and any rice for that matter, needs the proper amounts of spice, heat, and love. When you have too much of one thing and not enough of the other, it falls short. While my Abuela Lela rarely told me that she loved me, she showed me she loved me by the way she lived her life and by cooking the best rice ever, overflowing with love and care.

I'm telling you this story because in just the way rice needs the correct amounts of spice, heat, and love to come out right, we change makers, particularly Latinas and all women of color, need certain conditions for success. Amiga, you owe it to yourself and to your family, coworkers, and community partners to seek out the conditions in which you have the greatest likelihood for success. Because of this, we need you and your organization to make necessary changes so you can thrive in the fight for social, economic, political, and racial justice.

Do you wish you could have a greater impact on the world?

Do you wish that you could fight for justice *and* have a balanced, healthy life?

Do you find yourself doing behind-the-scenes, often invisible and unpaid, work?

Do you find yourself doing more than your share of the emotional labor in your organization, family, community?

Are you successfully building power in your own community but wrestling with how to work in successful cross-racial solidarity space?

The key to growing your impact and success is found in assessing and readjusting the ingredients in your life as you learn how to thrive in the fight for change. I invite you to consider how you can thrive in the fight. You can do this by learning how to Lead into your vision, Live into your fullest self, and Love past the negatives that hold you back; you can learn how to not just survive, but thrive. Remember, you can tell when you're surrendering in the fight for change when you find yourself Wishing for a different version of reality, Wondering where your own limits are, and Waiting for permission or answers to come from others.

My sister, you can make sure you're being set up (or setting yourself up) for success when you have equal doses of responsibility, resources, recognition, and room for reflection. This will help you create conditions for a more sustainable life that will allow you to show up as your most creative self. You can learn how to successfully integrate family and work, not feel like you always have to choose one over the other. The last thing we want to do is commit ourselves to a fight for freedom that our children, families, and friends grow to despise.

You can learn to lead from the front and more effectively disrupt anti-Black sentiment in your culture of origin so that you can build stronger multiracial relationships of trust and love. You can learn to lead from your purpose. You can trust your instincts and lean into them instead of tamping them down. Finally, you have the capacity to bring many more resources to bear for the fights you are leading. You have superpowers you're not yet fully using. You also have people around you who can't see their own giftedness. You can help them see their own reflection more clearly.

You have the ability to shape a generation of change makers with your talent, your vision, your hope and love. The organizations you help lead can learn a lot if they listen to you and center your leadership. You can help them do this if you choose. Or you can find or make a new space for your bad self!

Take One Step Today

Now that you've finished this book, I'm sure you feel like a lot has come at you. So, can I suggest that you consider taking one first step today? Look back at the three things in ninety days worksheet in chapter 3 and think about one area of your public leadership where you want to move from Surrender to Thrive. Make a commitment to yourself. Share it with an accountability partner. And set a time now to meet with them in ninety days to review your progress.

You and your movement can be more effective, have greater impact, and make better collective decisions.

How do I know this?

Because I see you.

The work you do is critical and necessary. And we need you to thrive in the fight for change.

Because I've been in the arena struggling with sweat, dirt, and blood on my face, I know how you feel. There have been times when I have led from the fullest version of myself and times, not so much. Sister, we all fall down, but it's how you get up that matters.

The approaches laid out in this book focus on both you and your organization. Please know, the work of changing our movement for social change is not all on you. It's on all of us. It's on all the people who read or recommend this book to others. It's on all of us who envision a future reality that is more beautiful than the one we currently see.

This world needs you. It needs your vision, your courage and leadership. If you choose to embark on this journey of deep reflection and exploration of your leadership, we all benefit.

Just imagine what would happen if communities across race and culture were to act together as one, even in one community. Imagine how our communities could change for the better. If we change this, we can change the whole game. This could spur a dynamic shift not only for Latinx communities, but for the entire movement for social change.

You hold the keys, sister, now turn on the engine and let's drive to a new future.

¡Adelante!

NOTES

FOREWORD

1   Paulette Beete, "#WisdomWednesday: Elizabeth Acevedo," *Art Works* (blog), National Endowment for the Arts, October 3, 2018, *https:// www.arts.gov/art-works/2018/wisdomwednesday-elizabeth-acevedo*.

INTRODUCTION

1   Ellie Buteau, "Reflecting on Leadership Diversity in Today's Nonprofit Sector," Center for Effective Philanthropy, September 5, 2019, *https://cep.org/reflecting-on-leadership-diversity-in-todays -nonprofit-sector/*.

2   United States Census Bureau, "Hispanic Heritage Month 2019," August 20, 2019, *https://www.census.gov/newsroom/facts-for -features/2019/hispanic-heritage-month.html#:~:text=59.9% 20million&text=Hispanics%20constituted%2018.3%25%20of%20the %20nation's%20total%20population*.

3   Tema Okun, "Manifestations of White Supremacy Culture," in *Dismantling Racism: A Workbook for Social Change Groups* (online workbook), accessed April 8, 2020, *http://www.dismantlingracism .org/white-supremacy-culture.html*. This piece on white supremacy culture is written by Tema Okun and builds on the work of many people, including (but not limited to) Andrea Ayvazian, Bree Carlson, Beverly Daniel Tatum, Eli Dueker, Nancy Emond, Jonn Lunsford, Sharon Martinas, Joan Olsson, David Rogers, James Williams, Sally Yee, as well as the work of Grassroots Leadership, Equity Institute Inc., the People's Institute for Survival and Beyond, the Challenging White Supremacy workshop, the Lillie Allen Institute, the Western States Center, and the contributions of hundreds of participants in the DR process.

4   Steve Phillips, *Brown Is the New White: How the Demographic Revolution Has Created a New American Majority* (New York: The New Press, 2016), 78.

5   Amy Tan, *The Valley of Amazement* (New York: HarperCollins, 2013),
    803, Kindle.

CHAPTER 1

1   Thomas L. Friedman, *Thank You for Being Late: An Optimist's Guide
    to Thriving in the Age of Accelerations* (New York: Farrar, Straus and
    Giroux, 2016), Blinkist.

CHAPTER 2

1   Tema Okun, "Manifestations of White Supremacy Culture," in *Dis-
    mantling Racism: A Workbook for Social Change Groups* (online work-
    book), accessed April 8, 2020, *http://www.dismantlingracism.org/
    white-supremacy-culture.html*. This piece on white supremacy culture
    is written by Tema Okun and builds on the work of many people,
    including (but not limited to) Andrea Ayvazian, Bree Carlson, Beverly
    Daniel Tatum, Eli Dueker, Nancy Emond, Jonn Lunsford, Sharon Mar-
    tinas, Joan Olsson, David Rogers, James Williams, Sally Yee, as well as
    the work of Grassroots Leadership, Equity Institute Inc., the People's
    Institute for Survival and Beyond, the Challenging White Supremacy
    workshop, the Lillie Allen Institute, the Western States Center, and the
    contributions of hundreds of participants in the DR process.

2   "Our Principles of Unity 2020," Mijente, accessed June 17, 2020,
    https://mijente.net/our-dna/.

3   Eduardo Briceño, "How to Get Better at the Things You Care About,"
    filmed November 2016 in Manhattan Beach, CA, TED video, *https://
    www.ted.com/talks/eduardo_briceno_how_to_get_better_at_the
    _things_you_care_about?language=en*.

CHAPTER 3

1   *Fulfilling America's Future: Latinas in the U.S., 2015*, US Department
    of Education (Washington, DC: GPO, 2015), 2.

2   "ACS Demographic and Housing Survey," United States Census
    Bureau, accessed July 5, 2020, *https://data.census.gov/cedsci/table
    ?q=hispanic%20or%20latino%20by%20state&hidePreview=false
    &tid=ACSDP1Y2018.DP05&t=Hispanic%20or%20Latino*.

3   "New National Poll Shows Biden, Sanders, O'Rourke, and Castro Ahead with Latino Voters in Lead Up to 2020," Latino Decisions, accessed April 8, 2020, *https://latinodecisions.com/blog/new -national-poll-shows-biden-sanders-orourke-and-castro-ahead -with-latino-voters-in-lead-up-to-2020/.*

4   "Univisión National Poll of Latino Registered Voters," Latino Decisions, June 2019, *http://publications.unidosus.org/bitstream /handle/123456789/1996/TheStateoftheLatinoVote.pdf?sequence=1 &isAllowed=y.*

5   Stuart Anderson, "The Most Inspiring Immigration Stories of 2019," *Forbes*, December 11, 2019, *https://www.forbes.com/sites /stuartanderson/2019/12/11/the-most-inspiring-immigration -stories-of-2019/#9c8f7cb15c60.*

6   "Univisión National Poll of Latino Registered Voters," Latino Decisions, September 2019, *http://publications.unidosus.org/bitstream /handle/123456789/1996/TheStateoftheLatinoVote.pdf?sequence =1&isAllowed=y.*

7   "Who Leads Us," Reflective Democracy Campaign, accessed July 5, 2020, *https://wholeads.us/electedofficials/.*

8   Johana Bencomo, telephone interview by author, April 2020.

9   Olivia Fox Cabane, *The Charisma Myth: How Anyone Can Master the Art and Science of Personal Magnetism* (New York: Penguin Group, 2012), Blinkist.

10 Amy Cuddy, "Your Body Language May Shape Who You Are," filmed June 2012 in Edinburgh, Scotland, TED video, *https://www.ted.com /talks/amy_cuddy_your_body_language_may_shape_who_you _are?language=en.*

11 "Jennifer Lopez Falls at AMAs 2009," YouTube video, posted by "pasathai99," November 21, 2010, *https://www.youtube.com/watch?v =KRTMAL7HB2k.*

12 "The Best of American Music Awards: JLo Falls and Bounces on Her Bottom & Will.I.Am Gives Play by Play," BlackTree TV, YouTube video, October 9, 2018, *https://www.youtube.com/watch?v =zwInmfwGQYM.*

CHAPTER 4

1   Nate Cohn, "More Hispanics Declaring Themselves White," *New York Times*, May 24, 2014, *https://www.nytimes.com/2014/05/22/upshot /more-hispanics-declaring-themselves-white.html*.

2   Isabel Wilkerson, *Caste: The Origin of our Discontents* (New York, Random House, 2020).

3   Natalia M. Perez, "On Generational Shame: Why Many Latinos Won't Admit They're Black, Too," *Natalia M. Perez* (blog), August 7, 2019, *https://www.nataliamperez.com/blog/generationalshame*.

4   Brené Brown, *Rising Strong: How the Ability to Reset Transforms the Way We Live, Love, Parent and Lead* (New York: Random House, 2017), 45.

5   Denise Collazo and Stephanie Valencia, "Latinos Must Acknowledge Our Own Racism, Then We Must Pledge to Fight It," *Miami Herald*, June 10, 2020, *https://www.miamiherald.com/opinion/op-ed /article243375201.html*.

6   Ibram X. Kendi, *How to Be an Antiracist* (New York: One World, 2019), 235.

7   Associated Press, "136 Variations of Brazilian Skin Colors," trans. Lilia Moritz Schwarcz, ed. Achal Prabhala, *USA Today*, July 8, 2014, *https://www.usatoday.com/story/sports/soccer/2014/07/08/136 -variations-of-brazilian-skin-colors/12373343/*.

8   Gabriela Mernin, Hunter College High School, "99 Problems: Shades of Belonging," *New York Daily News*, November 3, 2016, *https://www .nydailynews.com/new-york/education/examining-paper-bag-test -evolved-article-1.2844394*.

9   Pablo Pardo, "El Voto Ignorado de los Latinos en EEUU," *El Mundo Internacional*, June 28, 2019, *https://www.elmundo.es/internacional /2019/06/28/5d14c85521efa022388b45dd.html*.

10 Stephanie Valencia et al., "Hispanics in America Are Under Attack," *The Washington Post*, August 6, 2019, *https://www.washingtonpost .com/opinions/call-the-el-paso-shooting-what-it-is-domestic -terrorism-against-the-hispanic-community/2019/08/06/c8674e1c -b7a9-11e9-a091-6a96e67d9cce_story.html*.

11 "Resources," Black Lives Matter, accessed June 22, 2020, *https:// blacklivesmatter.com/resources/*.

12   Tatum Dorrell, Matt Herndon, and Jourdan Dorrell, "Antiracist Allyship Starter Pack," Ally.tools, accessed August 5, 2020, *https://docs.google.com/spreadsheets/u/1/d/e/2PACX-1vTkmrhfhYUfCcTbp3NoDmxKZUAN7xMiVuhqIlNBizKz-Ih7yPPqTPFgYzmd5NgKtEdpVugB6GoZwPWR/pubhtml.*

13   Denise Collazo, "Noticing, Naming, and Disrupting Anti-Blackness in Your Culture of Origin," Denise Collazo (website), September 4, 2020, *https://denisecollazo.com/.*

CHAPTER 5

1   Kim Yi Dionne, "Amílcar Cabral's Life as a Pan-Africanist, Anti-Colonial Revolutionary Still Inspires," *Washington Post*, June 21, 2019, *https://www.washingtonpost.com/politics/2019/06/21/amlcar-cabrals-life-pan-africanist-anti-colonial-revolutionary-still-inspires-today/.*

2   Abby Aguirre, "Octavia Butler's Prescient Vision of a Zealot Elected to 'Make America Great Again,'" *New Yorker*, July 26, 2017, *https://www.newyorker.com/books/second-read/octavia-butlers-prescient-vision-of-a-zealot-elected-to-make-america-great-again.*

3   Nikole Hannah-Jones, "Our Democracy's Founding Ideals Were False When They Were Written. Black Americans Have Fought to Make Them True," 1619 Project of *New York Times Magazine*, August 18, 2019.

4   David A. Thomas and Robin J. Ely, "Making Differences Matter: A New Paradigm for Managing Diversity," *Harvard Business Review*, September-October 1996, *https://hbr.org/1996/09/making-differences-matter-a-new-paradigm-for-managing-diversity.*

5   Vivian Hunt, et al., *Delivering through Diversity*, McKinsey & Company, January 2018, *https://www.mckinsey.com/~/media/McKinsey/Business%20Functions/Organization/Our%20Insights/Delivering%20through%20diversity/Delivering-through-diversity_full-report.ashx.*

6   Angela Aguirre, "How I Define My Chingona Fire," Huff Post, January 25, 2017, *https://www.huffpost.com/entry/how-i-define-my-chingona-fire_b_5887de69e4b0a53ed60c6a35.*

CHAPTER 6

1   Arik Chokey, "Campaign Cash in Florida's 2018 Race for Governor," *South Florida Sentinel*, November 7, 2018, *https://projects.sun -sentinel.com/fl-governor-race-cash/*.

CONCLUSION

1   Robert Zemeckis, *Forrest Gump* (1994; Hollywood, CA: Paramount Pictures, 1994, 1:19).

GLOSSARY OF SPANISH WORDS

Abuela: Grandma

Abuelas, tías, hermanas, and madres: Grandmothers, aunts, sisters, and mothers

Adelante: Forward

Afro-Boricua: Puerto Ricans who identify as Black and Puerto Rican

Afro-Cubana: Cuban women who identify as Black and Cuban

Afro-Latina: Latina women who identify as Black and Latina

Amiga: Female friend

Arroz con gandules, arroz con camarones, arroz con jueyes, arroz con pollo, arroz con habichuelas, arroz con salchicha, arroz blanco, asopao, paella, and the Christmas classic arroz con dulce: Rice with pigeon peas, rice with shrimp, rice with crabmeat, rice with chicken, rice with beans, rice with Vienna sausage, white rice, rice stew, seafood rice stew, and sweet rice

Bizabuelita: Great-grandma

Boricua: Name for Puerto Ricans derived from the native Arawak term Boriken, which means "land of the noble lords"

Chicano: Americans of Mexican descent

Chingonas: An informal term used by Mexican and other Latinx people to refer to bad ass women

Cocineras: Cooks

Comadre: Close, respected female friend

El nene lindo: The beautiful one

Elotes: Corn on the cob

Hermana: Sister

Latina: Latino woman

Mentoras: Mentors

Mestizo: Sometimes used to refer to the Hispanic culture of the Americas (as it is a mix of different Indigenous, European, and African cultures)

Mi hermana: My sister

Mija: My daughter

Mujer: Woman

Mujeres: Women

Paletas: Frozen pops

Sofrito: Base of spices that serve as the central ingredients for most Puerto Rican cooking

Somos más y no tenemos miedo: There are more of us and we're not afraid

Taino: Original inhabitants of Puerto Rico who derive from the Arawak Native people

Telenovela: Spanish-language soap opera

Tía: Aunt

Un caldero de arroz: A pot of rice

RESOURCES

Here is a card for you to cut out and carry with you.

FIVE SYMPTOMS OF WHITE SUPREMACY IN INSTITUTIONS

➥ individualism

➥ fear of failure

➥ fear of open conflict

➥ binary thinking

➥ right to comfort (for some)

Credit: *Dismantling Racism*, Tema Okun

ACKNOWLEDGMENTS

M y beautiful mother, Carmen Berrios Padín, has taught me how a busy working mom can love God and love others. Momma, you have always pointed me toward God and toward truth. You truly love your neighbor as you love yourself and invite me to be the best version of myself. Also, thanks for reading every single word of this book and helping with proofreading. Thanks to my Daddy, Rafael Enrique Padín, who's always been like a second mom to me—strong, tender, vulnerable, and hilarious. Momma, you taught me to look up; Daddy, you taught me to look around.

To my husband, best friend, and partner in life, Julio Cesar Collazo, thank you for all the days and nights you sacrificed so that this book could emerge. Thanks for all the coffee, water, French fries, oatmeal, and even clean laundry that magically appeared while I was writing. You are my media naranja and I'm eager for all of the adventures the next thirty years will bring.

To my daughter Elisa Marie, you have grown my heart and become the kind of woman I want to be friends with. Your brave posture toward life inspires me and everyone else around you. Keep laughing and creating, my sweet Bebé. To my grandbaby Leyla Rose Delgado, you are a healer and you have been since before you were born; Weewa loves you! I love all of you more than you could ever know.

To my comadre Andrea Marta, thank you for always being there to listen, encourage, cry, and laugh with me. Thanks for being my ride or die. You have taught me so much about how to be the best organizer and best person I can be. To Tatiana, thanks for helping me choose the title and cover art for the book. Love to Yahir and my godson Jair(cito) for teaching me important lessons about discipline that helped me write this book. Nina loves you all.

I am deeply grateful to Rev. Alvin Herring, executive director of Faith in Action, for sharing your ideas, music, family, stories, and vision with me. You have modeled for me what it means to show up as your full self. You lead us with the perfect mix of strength and vulnerability. Working with you has been one of the highlights of my career. Thank you for all your support and encouragement as this book was being written. Love to you and Debbie from Julio and me.

The following leaders served on the Thriving in the Fight Advisory Board. You all inspired, coached, encouraged, and supported me every single step of the way. Though it bears my name, this book belongs to all of you Alpha Chingonxs!

Johana Bencomo	Catalina Morales
Heather Cabral	Richard Morales
Tere Flores Onofre	Nanci Palacios
Brenda Gavin-García	Gabby Trejo
Denise López	Crystal Walthall
Andrea Marta	Erin Williams

Thank you to the many community organizers, leaders, professors, and book doulas who cheered me on and helped make this work better by reading even the earliest of drafts.

Margie Alt	Dr. Stacy Blake-Beard
Dr. Lonce Bailey	Carmen Cancel
Michael Bell	Lucy Flores

Becca Guerra

Alia Harvey-Quinn

Ivy Hest

Phyllis Hill

Brittany Hughes

Jim Keddy

Gail Lang

Chevalier Lovett

Dr. Kristen Lynch

Josie Mooney

Isabelle Moses

Socorro Ramos-Aviles

Evelyn Rangel

Cortney Sanders

Sarah Silva

Kelly Weigel

Erica Williams

Rev. Jennifer Jones, I thank you for hearing and loving me when I was at my most shrill and least lovable. Rev. Michael-Ray Mathews, thank you for wrestling with me over time and offering me the grace to reinvent relationship with you.

Thanks to Eugene Eric Kim for inviting me into a community of collaborative practitioners, and for connecting me with Yi Zhang from the Berrett-Koehler Foundation. Steve Piersanti at Berrett-Koehler Publishers has been my trail-guide, encourager, truth-teller, and advocate since this process began. Thanks, Steve, for helping an oak tree emerge from an acorn. Valerie Caldwell from Berrett-Koehler used her influence to advocate for this book cover when others couldn't yet see its magic.

Shout-out to Gabrielle Dolan, who encouraged me to share my ideas with others, and for introducing me to Kelly Irving, who broke the book-writing process down into bite-sized pieces. I'm grateful to Ana Teresa Rodriguez, the talented artist who illustrated the book cover. Follow her on Instagram at @artexanateresa. Susan Berge, copy editor extraordinaire, I'd work with you anywhere, anytime!

Thanks to all of you who have sponsored house meetings and events to share this book's message. I am grateful you have chosen to buy this book and encourage others to do the same. You are contributing to the movement for social change by reading the book, but also with your purchase. The net proceeds from the sale of this book will go to a fund designated to support Latina organizers.

Blessings and love to you all! I wish you strength in the journey, hope in battle, and power to thrive in the fight.

INDEX

Latinas, and women of color more broadly, are closest to injustice and are best suited to provide just solutions.

Denise Collazo is squarely focused on encouraging women of color to lead into their vision, live into their fullest selves, and love past negatives that too often hold them back. She is a gifted speaker who leaves listeners compelled to take action on how they can act on their purpose. She mentors, coaches, and raises funds in collaboration with other women to find the just solutions we so desperately need. By doing this, she models what a woman working with and for women really looks like.

She's as comfortable speaking with people in their living room or front porch as she is meeting with national political and corporate leaders to advance social change for families. This is a gift she was given by her ancestors.

Denise is the senior advisor for external affairs and director of institutional advancement at Faith in Action (formerly PICO National Network), the nation's largest faith-based, progressive organizing network, where she has advanced the cause of social justice over the past twenty-five years. As senior advisor she represents Faith in Action with foundation and corporate executives, builds strategic partnerships with organizational executives across the movement for change, and is crafting a national individual membership program to expand Faith in Action to all fifty states.

She has served as community organizer at Oakland Community Organizations; executive director of what is now called Faith in Action Bay Area; and Faith in Action national director of development, national deputy director, and national chief of staff. She began her advocacy career in Washington, DC, as a fellow at the National Puerto Rican Coalition and program associate for Community Change.

She is a graduate of Harvard University, where she studied Romance language and literature and completed all the requirements for pre-medicine. Her thesis, written in Spanish, explored the role of the Taino people in Puerto Rican literature across time.

Denise attended the Harvard Kennedy School Executive Education Women and Power program, where she partnered with fifty international leaders across sectors. She is an official member of the Forbes Nonprofit Council, an invitation-only organization for executives in successful nonprofit organizations.

Denise has led successful advocacy campaigns to win valuable, lasting change in people's lives, including better housing, improved transit, and better wages. In 2002, she led her organization to run a local ballot measure for affordable housing. This effort served as one of the first Faith in Action attempts to influence policy via voting. In 2012, she led the successful Florida statewide No on 3 campaign to stop a dangerous revenue measure that would have decimated funding for vulnerable families. In 2016 she led the national Together We Vote campaign, which held 829,000 conversations with Black, Latinx, and Asian and Pacific Islander voters, who are regularly ignored by campaigns and candidates. She helped lay the early groundwork for the 2018 Florida Yes on 4 campaign to restore voting rights to people returning from incarceration. The measure eventually passed under the leadership of Desmond Meade and Pastor Rhonda Walker-Thomas.

Denise may be able to help you grow your leadership via:

- ➤ Mentoring and impact coaching for leaders of color
- ➤ Providing technical support for action-oriented senior executives to center the leadership of Black and Brown women
- ➤ Creating sustainable organizational structures that help employees better integrate family and work and grow their creativity
- ➤ Developing culturally competent, strategic community organizing plans

Denise enjoys sharing her thoughts about community organizing with a particular focus on women's leadership. Her work has been featured in CNN.com, the *Miami Herald*, the *Chronicle of Philanthropy*, *Nonprofit Quarterly*, and Forbes Nonprofit Council.

She refills her tank by riding her bike, going to the beach, and reading. Denise is married to the love of her life, Julio Cesar Collazo. Her daughter Elisa and grandbaby Leyla Rose are the sparkle in her eye.

Visit her website at *www.DeniseCollazo.com*.

Berrett–Koehler
Publishers

Berrett-Koehler is an independent publisher dedicated to an ambitious mission: *Connecting people and ideas to create a world that works for all.*

Our publications span many formats, including print, digital, audio, and video. We also offer online resources, training, and gatherings. And we will continue expanding our products and services to advance our mission.

We believe that the solutions to the world's problems will come from all of us, working at all levels: in our society, in our organizations, and in our own lives. Our publications and resources offer pathways to creating a more just, equitable, and sustainable society. They help people make their organizations more humane, democratic, diverse, and effective (and we don't think there's any contradiction there). And they guide people in creating positive change in their own lives and aligning their personal practices with their aspirations for a better world.

And we strive to practice what we preach through what we call "The BK Way." At the core of this approach is *stewardship,* a deep sense of responsibility to administer the company for the benefit of all of our stakeholder groups, including authors, customers, employees, investors, service providers, sales partners, and the communities and environment around us. Everything we do is built around stewardship and our other core values of *quality, partnership, inclusion,* and *sustainability.*

This is why Berrett-Koehler is the first book publishing company to be both a B Corporation (a rigorous certification) and a benefit corporation (a for-profit legal status), which together require us to adhere to the highest standards for corporate, social, and environmental performance. And it is why we have instituted many pioneering practices (which you can learn about at www.bkconnection.com), including the Berrett-Koehler Constitution, the Bill of Rights and Responsibilities for BK Authors, and our unique Author Days.

We are grateful to our readers, authors, and other friends who are supporting our mission. We ask you to share with us examples of how BK publications and resources are making a difference in your lives, organizations, and communities at www.bkconnection.com/impact.

Dear reader,

Thank you for picking up this book and welcome to the worldwide BK community! You're joining a special group of people who have come together to create positive change in their lives, organizations, and communities.

What's BK all about?

Our mission is to connect people and ideas to create a world that works for all.

Why? Our communities, organizations, and lives get bogged down by old paradigms of self-interest, exclusion, hierarchy, and privilege. But we believe that can change. That's why we seek the leading experts on these challenges—and share their actionable ideas with you.

A welcome gift

To help you get started, we'd like to offer you a **free copy** of one of our bestselling ebooks:

www.bkconnection.com/welcome

When you claim your **free ebook**, you'll also be subscribed to our blog.

Our freshest insights

Access the best new tools and ideas for leaders at all levels on our blog at ideas.bkconnection.com.

Sincerely,

Your friends at Berrett-Koehler